ENCOUNTERS

Experiences with Nonhuman Intelligences

ALSO BY D. W. PASULKA

American Cosmic: UFOs, Religion, Technology
Heaven Can Wait: Purgatory in Catholic Devotional
and Popular Culture

ENCOUNTERS

Experiences with Nonhuman Intelligences

D. W. Pasulka

ST. MARTIN'S
ESSENTIALS
NEW YORK

First published in the United States by St. Martin's Essentials,
an imprint of St. Martin's Publishing Group

www.stmartins.com

Designed by Steven Seighman

The Library of Congress Cataloging-in-Publication Data is available
upon request.

ISBN 978-1-250-87956-1 (hardcover)
ISBN 978-1-250-87957-8 (ebook)

Our books may be purchased in bulk for promotional, educational, or busi-
ness use. Please contact your local bookseller or the Macmillan Corporate and
Premium Sales Department at 1-800-221-7945, extension 5442, or by email at
MacmillanSpecialMarkets@macmillan.com.

First Edition: 2023

10 9 8 7 6 5 4 3 2 1

CONTENTS

Introduction 1

1. The Space Psychologist...19

2. Technology and AI: A Language Bridge Back to Contact 46

3. The Gray Man...62

4. Gray Man II 84

5. The Soldier...103

6. Gnosis 121

7. Moon Girl...141

8. Children of the Invisibles 173

9. From Atheism to a Magical Mystery Tour 197

10. The Dream Network: Dreamscapes, Visions, and Lucid Dreams ...215

Conclusion: The End of an Allegory............................237

Acknowledgments...241

Notes 243

INTRODUCTION

Though many may not believe, the truth is already here.

—KITE (SUZANNE KITE), OGLÁLA LAKȞÓTA

The path to writing about UFOs was unexpected but none-theless a natural progression of my research. As a professor of the history of religion, I study reports of miraculous events and afterlife worlds in Christian history. This includes sightings of aerial beings of light, miraculous flying houses (that's right), monks and nuns who levitate and bilocate, and a religious doctrine called purgatory. I relate this because my work reveals how people's beliefs often emerge from their interactions with places and their exposure to media. Scholars in my field generally do not weigh in on the truth or falsity of religious claims to truth. Instead, we study the social effects of religious belief and practice. When I finished my work on the Catholic tradition, the shift to the study of UFO cultures seemed straightforward. Belief in UFOs, I wrote, is a rapidly growing spirituality that corresponds to the twenty-first-century shift to digital infrastructures. It is similar to religion because people see things in the sky, aerial objects, and they have had no physical evidence that they exist, yet they often attribute to them a spiritual significance. UFOs are, as Carl Jung famously wrote, "technological angels." They are symbols and signs of a new epoch in human history.

The story of UFOs, however, turned out to be more complicated than I'd thought. In short order I found myself among scientists of aeronautics and space travel, experiencers—people who believe they are in contact with extraterrestrials—as well as various agents of intelligence communities, and countless journalists and media personalities. I developed friendships with many of them. The scientists with whom I worked were at the top of their fields—experts in biomedical technologies. They believed they had evidence that UFOs were real. I began to understand that the UFO event was a spiritual reality for many people, including these scientists, and even though I didn't know it at the time, the topic of my research was just about to get *very real*.

Through my study I found several things to be the case, which I detailed in my published research. First, the public perception of UFOs is mediated and often managed by media and agents of (dis)information.[1] Second, the claims of some of the people in my study—that they studied UFOs and that the study of UFOs has been ongoing since the 1940s—*turned out to be true*. I didn't believe or disbelieve the claims made by the scientists in my study. Instead, I documented the development of what I believed is a new form of religion or religious expression. I was as surprised, as were many people, when the United States military and the Pentagon, in the summer of 2021, released an unclassified report that acknowledged that they had funded secret programs to study UFOs. Finally, this development pushed me to think beyond my training and the resources available in my field. In effect, the Pentagon report (*Preliminary Assessment: Unidentified Aerial Phenomena*) ratified this new form of religion and spirituality.[2]

We are currently at a fork in the road with respect to how UFOs are interpreted. The history of religions suggests that, with respect to new religious expressions, the creation of state-sponsored religious institutions often trump people's lived experiences, usually through suppression and silence. Since the UFO is often interpreted in spiritual and religious ways, we can expect to see the same process at play. The early Christian Gnostics saw their books banned and declared heretical by the newly institutionalized Christian church in Rome, for example. The question I posed to myself, before writing this book, was: What, and whose, stories about UFOs are being silenced today? I didn't pose this question for wholly altruistic reasons. The question would help me define the streams that are most revolutionary about this nascent religiosity.

THE WITNESSES

Among the people who study UFOs, one stood out to me as possessing an effective method of research, and he was far removed from the field of religious studies. Dr. Jacques Vallée has a PhD in information science from Northwestern University, is trained in astrophysics, and has worked extensively in the field of technology for the United States

Department of Defense. He was a close associate and colleague of Dr. J. Allen Hynek, who was a longtime consultant for the United States Air Force on topics related to UFOs, and a key figure in most of the secret programs involved in UFO research. Vallée maintains a career as a well-known and successful venture capitalist and calls his work in the field of UFOs a hobby. His focus on witness testimonies and his recognition of potential disinformation is invaluable in the assessment of UFO cases and their social repercussions. I found that academics generally will not approach the topic of secrecy and disinformation related to UFOs. This is understandable as UFO disinformation is a murky topic that is difficult to understand. Yet secrecy and disinformation have been an intrinsic feature of the history of UFOs in the United States, so it is unavoidable. Responsible research into this topic must address disinformation. To avoid it is to avoid the totality of the topic. Jacques not only practices sound research but he also incorporates knowledge of how disinformation works, and this is a necessary tool in the tool kit of the researcher who endeavors to study UFOs.

Jacques wrote that the best way to study this phenomenon is to do field research, that is, to talk to witnesses and to visit the sites where UFOs are seen. It may seem simple, but this method has not dominated official or academic studies:

> The only way we're going to understand it is to stop talking to each other, and go back and talk to the witnesses. So, I put the highest priority on first-hand cases that had not been reported to the press or to the

UFO community, because the moment the cases become part of ongoing discussion, they get polarized:
the witnesses are bombarded with all kinds of questions; there are biases; the ego gets into it. I wanted to
do a quiet kind of long-term research.[3]

What do the witnesses have to say? Generally, not what
most people assume. In the interviews and talks that came
after the publication of my research, it became clear to me
that nonwitnesses have a view of contact that is informed
by entertainment media—books, television, and popular
culture. Their version of contact envisions a scenario in
which nonhuman and extraterrestrial intelligence contact
humans through beings that look humanlike and drive
spaceships that resemble flying sports cars.

In interviews I fielded questions and comments such as,
"Why don't aliens land on the White House lawn?" or, "I
can't wait until ET asks to meet our leaders." In comparison
with witness reports, the prevailing idea of contact held by
most people is unlike that which I heard from witnesses.
Jacques also wrote about the narrow ways in which UFO
events are interpreted and framed by media. Author Whitley Strieber's book *Communion* came out in the 1980s. It is
a harrowing tale of his own experience with beings he calls
"the visitors." The cover of the book features the image of
what has come to be the iconic look of an alien being, with
large almond-shaped eyes and greenish reptilian skin. The
image pervaded culture to the extent that Jacques noticed
that if witness stories did not conform to the look of Strieber's

alien, researchers discounted their reports. Media shapes how people view contact and determines how they envision UFO contact scenarios.

Researchers tend to focus on UFO events either as the appearance of advanced technologies *or* they focus entirely on the subjective experiences of the person who encounters alleged spacecraft or extraterrestrials. Yet many witness reports show that these positions are not mutually exclusive. When people see what appear to be unexplained aerial objects, they also experience realities that are not compatible with their ordinary reality. Additionally, there are aftershocks to these effects. People report episodes of knowing the future—or precognition—and other nonordinary effects. Rather than treat these experiences as nonrational and paranormal (in the sense of being strange), these events and effects can be understood by a shift in perspective for which there are precedents in religious traditions and within the lore of indigenous cultures.

When Harvard researcher Dr. John Mack published his classic book *Abduction: Human Encounters with Aliens* in the 1990s, his research focused on the initial shock that normal people have when they experience what they interpret as being in contact with either extraterrestrial or nonhuman intelligences. His research moved on from this initial shock, however, and he came to realize that most of human societies have recognized that people have these experiences. He learned that the knowledge systems of many indigenous cultures possess frameworks for understanding contact. They do not pathologize these events or experiences. Lakota are among the many indigenous cultures that report contact with members of "Star Nations," or what others would call extraterrestrials. The realities of this contact are enfolded into a worldview in which "the distinction between natural and supernatural, so basic to European thought, was meaningless."[4]

In 2018, an illuminating exchange occurred that shed light on the difference between the prevailing and dominant idea of UFOs and that of the lore contained within some indigenous cultures. It was a conversation between scholars of indigenous studies and the Breakthrough Listen Initiative of SETI, the Search for Extraterrestrial Intelligence. SETI reached out to the group and asked them to produce a statement in answer to the question, "What would you want SETI scientists to know about potentially making contact?" The scholars were impressed that SETI had reached out to them, and they diligently set to work. Soon, however, in conversations with the scientists at SETI, they reported that SETI had instructed them to keep their statement to two pages "to avoid all commentary about whether contact had already begun."[5] The scholars of indigenous studies, who are from indigenous communities, would not misrepresent their cultural knowledge, so they spoke up and explained that for them, contact has been an ongoing reality. The Breakthrough Listen Initiative, through their actions, seemed to discount that contact is an ongoing reality for many people from indigenous cultures around the world. Contact with nonhuman intelligence has also been an ongoing reality attested to within almost every traditional religion. Yet SETI does not acknowledge the information gained within these traditions. *Why?*

Just as in the case of the people who asked me why ET hadn't landed on the White House lawn (ironically, UFOs *did* buzz the skies over the White House in 1952), it appears that SETI and many people have a specific idea of contact that is informed by media. If data emerges that contradicts this belief or idea, they dismiss it. This is called "confirmation bias" and it plays a huge role in the public perception of UFO events. Some aspects of confirmation bias seem to be based on fear. I call this fear because many conversations I've had with government officials and journalists reveal that they believe that contact with nonhuman intelligence would eradicate the religious beliefs of billions of people and thus create social mayhem. It won't. Traditional religions, including Christianity, Islam, and Judaism, as well as Buddhism, and Hinduism, in addition to indigenous communities, include some recognition, in parts of their histories and traditions, either acknowledging or pondering the existence of extraterrestrials or nonhuman intelligence, or do not discount it.

The fear was made clear in an exchange I had with a scholar who studies how scenarios of UFO contact might affect members of religious traditions. He thought that this would eradicate people's belief in God and in an afterlife. My position is that it wouldn't impact religious belief, as religions already have in place metaphysical categories for nonhuman intelligences of many types (God, djinn, angels, beings from other planets, etc.). He answered my suggestion with a scenario. He suggested that contact with extraterrestrials would be a problem for monotheistic religions if aliens thousands of years ahead of humans landed on Earth and explained that there is no God. He said that humans would be inclined to believe the aliens because they possessed technology more advanced than human technology.

As I read this scenario it occurred to me that this looks like how colonists might view themselves if they engaged in self-reflection. What are we afraid of from contact? If we happen to be an empire, it appears that we are afraid of meeting beings much like ourselves. The fear of this particular contact scenario happens to be a narrative of colonization, imbued with violence and subjugation. It could possibly be true, but it is one of many interpretations of contact.

This military-empire scenario is just one view of many about UFO contact. Identified sky objects are as old as the human societies that have identified them. As I delved into the indigenous written and mostly oral cultural knowledge about extraterrestrials and nonhuman intelligence, I found a direct connection between these ideas and the experiences and beliefs of the scientists I knew who worked within the programs that studied this phenomenon. Ironically, the scientists who studied what they believed are UFOs do not have a military scenario of UFO contact, and, like the indigenous scholars who spoke with SETI, believe that we are already in contact. They do not posit contact as a future possibility, *but as a lived reality*.

In my previous research I used pseudonyms to protect the professional reputations of the scientists with whom I had worked. Since then, one of the scientists, Dr. Garry Nolan, dropped his pseudonym and went public. The other is still known through the pseudonym Tyler D. Each shares the belief that contact has happened and is ongoing.

Why assume, like members of SETI and other institutions,

that contact is only a future possibility? Perhaps, as Suzanne Kite writes, because it serves a particular agenda:

> The colonial sense of progress is indelibly fixed to an unrelenting linear timeline towards a settler future, where Indigenous peoples are the uncivilized past, American white-superiority the present, and Mars colonization and extraterrestrials the future.[6]

This is one fork in the road regarding UFO belief and it is a direction that we don't have to take. Assumptions of the most innovative of the scientists who study UFOs confers with the knowledge gleaned from indigenous communities' centuries of contact. The other fork in the road appears to point in the direction of a comparison between patterns shared by these communities. It is time to take Vallée's advice and turn back to the witnesses.

LISTENING TO PLACES: TERRESTRIAL, VIRTUAL, COSMIC

In my previous work two places instigated a transformation in my understanding of UFO religiosity. The first was New Mexico, and specifically San Augustin, where I visited the location of an alleged UFO crash-debris site that was reported to be among a flap of sightings and crashes that occurred in 1947. This was, obviously, a highly mythic and mythologized place, inextricably bound to the atomic bomb and military secrecy, as well as being the ground-zero location for UFO belief. I ended that research at the Vatican and Specola Vaticana—the Vatican Observatory—two other highly mythologized places and sites at the apex of Western religious and colonial culture. I could not have orchestrated, even if I had tried, a more fitting arrangement of iconic geography in which to experience and write about the new global cosmism—the belief in the cosmic evolution of the human species. Place, and its relationship to beliefs and practices, more than ever, revealed itself as a primary site of revelation.

Places, not only specific places around the globe but the planet we live on—Earth—figure prominently in the ensuing chapters. Human beings are venturing into spaces they have never traveled. These spaces are virtual *and* cosmic. That human beings are visiting both places at the same time is historic and momentous. New places bring new ways of thinking and being, and we are only on the cusp of learning what these are and will become. In referencing "new forms of consciousness" arising from these spaces, I am not referring to a new-age idea like a coming Age of Aquarius. Instead, these observations come from my work with scholars who identify novel brain states and consciousnesses that are associated with space and virtual environments.

For example, Dr. Iya Whiteley is a space psychologist and a cognitive engineer who advised the UK Space Agency as a Chair of the Space Environment Working Group. She finds that in space, astronauts develop their own rules and culture, which is often at odds with and significantly deviates from the common rules assumed by people in mission control. Her work identifies the very beginnings of a shift in global consciousness with respect to space. Her research contributed to a shift in the culture of aviation. Her research helped eliminate the stigma associated with pilot reports of anomalous phenomena. Her current hobby focuses on helping pilots safely process anomalous phenomenon. Her work with pilots and astronauts, as well as her knowledge of indigenous practices of health and well-being, inspired her to create a program developing means of communication with intelligent nonhuman life that already surrounds us. She also creates technologies that she hopes will transcribe animal languages. She is among a growing number of scientists who utilize technology to decipher the languages of animals. Chapters 1 and 2 feature her work and projects.

The people featured in the following chapters are experiencers, that is, they report that they have experiences with nonhuman intelligence. The question is, Can this experience be called contact with extraterrestrial intelligence? This question is something that has not been answered in any conclusive way. Even the scientists I know who are most embedded within the current programs of UFO research do not answer this question, because they don't know. They are involved in space research and in the efforts to understand aerial objects within our atmosphere, and they believe that this intelligence is nonhuman and related to aerial vehicles that do not appear to be from Earth. But they also report other things, such as vivid dreams, nonlinear experiences of time, and knowing things that will happen. Often they will not officially report these aspects of their experiences because they do not fit the common perception of an extraterrestrial encounter. They report them to me, though, and to Dr. Whiteley. Researchers need to discard the mediated idea of extraterrestrial contact so that they can begin to understand the nature of contact with perceived nonhuman intelligence. Whatever it is called, whatever name it is given, it is a reality for many people and has been for many thousands of years.

After exploring Dr. Whiteley's work, chapters 3 and 4 relate the experiences of a scientist who works for a major research agency. He is pseudonymous due to the nature of his work. His experiences highlight religious and supernatural aspects of contact that are rarely addressed, which are the religious and spiritual experiences and interpretations that they often inspire. An important part of the study of UFO events are the spiritual and religious frameworks of the experiencers. By following the data, even if it is considered strange, we can approach cases with open-minded inquiry and include information that doesn't conform to previous assumptions. With the exponential rate of AI, we will be able to map and understand this data in ways that will help progress knowledge of these curious experiences.

Chapters 5 and 6 explore the experiences of Jose, a young soldier and former US Marine who understands UFOs within the context of his tumultuous upbringing in Texas and New Mexico. For him, UFO contact events are folded within a worldview permeated by spiritual forces, including *ángeles y demonios*—angels and demons. Jose's experiences also highlight a theme that emerges in many reports—the experience of an invisible network that is not the internet. Jose compares this organic network to the noösphere of Jesuit philosopher Pierre Teilhard de Chardin's writings, which he refers to as an Earth atmosphere of information. This concept shows up in Dr. Whiteley's work as well as within indigenous knowledge systems that link it with being in sync with land and place.

Chapter 7 extends what is known about contact with nonhuman intelligence into new frontiers. Simone is a venture capitalist who specializes in humane uses of AI and has worked on projects with DARPA, the Defense Advanced Research Projects Agency, which is a research and development agency of the United States Department of Defense responsible for the development of emerging technologies for use by the military. She proposes the bold hypothesis that aliens, or extraterrestrials, are now here on Earth and that they are from outside of space-time. They are not extraterrestrial beings from another galaxy, but nonhuman intelligence from outside of our dimension of space-time made explicit through AI. She supports this hypothesis with research and science. Additionally, in her work the organic network appears again as an inextricable aspect of contact. Simone also relates her experiences of contact within the framework of "the download," which was explored as something related to the scientists with whom I worked. This is a process through which extremely creative people appear to receive, through spontaneous cognition, calculations, information about biomedical products, or similar types of information without any apparent effort. Simone is one of a group of successful technologists who believe that AI will be sentient and that it represents humans from the future who many people interpret as aliens.

I've mentioned that among the people who showed up

within my research sphere as soon as I focused on the topics of UFOs included some members of intelligence communities. Government programs from the 1950s onward attempted to manage the public perception of UFOs, and now the United States government has admitted that it has been studying the topic. It makes sense that intelligence agents, whose job it is to collect information, would be interested in this research. Chapter 8 explores my relationships with some of the people I have met who are a part of these communities by choice, and some who are not. My colleague and friend, Patricia Turrisi, grew up with a father who worked for what she refers to as "the secret space program." Due to the nature of his work, she had an unusual childhood. I met many people who had similar experiences. This chapter is part interview and part reflection upon these lesser known realities of UFO cultures.

The final chapters relate the remarkable UFO experiences of former atheist Len Filppu. His encounter with a UFO as a teenager began a shift in his worldview that spanned the course of many years. His experiences reveal common themes among the experiences described within the pages of this book—dreams that are so vivid that these experiencers redefine them as visions; encounters with not only UFOs but other types of nonhuman intelligence; and strings of synchronicities or meaningful coincidences. I've ended the book with Len's experiences because they provide the clearest example of the UFO event I've encountered among thousands of accounts. It involves not just the event itself, but the context of the event and the ensuing effects on Len. Len started out as a committed atheist, yet his experiences were so meaningful and even unlikely that he came to an understanding that there is a higher power and a belief that life is intrinsically spiritual and meaningful. Len was not compelled by parents or society to come to this conclusion . . . and he didn't reach it on his own. He felt that he had direction. The direction was not from an individual but was revealed through meaningful events and unlikely occurrences that he felt revealed an inherent meaning to his life that he characterizes as magical and sacred.

A REORIENTATION

When I decided to study UFOs and the people who believed in them, I saw the UFO through stereotypes. I thought of them as flying saucers from planets in solar systems far, far away. Like most people, I inherited this view from movies, television, and video games. I didn't expect to meet scientists who lived like monks and mystics and believed that UFOs were interdimensional intelligences or emergent consciousness. I also didn't expect to hear reports of altered realities, uncanny coincidences, angels and demons, and the existence of a network like that described by Jesuit priest and scholar Teilhard de Chardin. According to these reports, this network predates the internet and is accessible to some people. All these elements, repeated over and over, convinced me that the UFO constitutes an ongoing event for many people of which the sighting is just one aspect. In addition to the sighting are many other elements. This book details the ongoing event of UFO contact, inclusive of the sighting but also of accompanying supernatural effects and events.

The reports suggest an emerging spiritual reorientation of global proportions. Jacques Vallée often states that the most significant aspect of the UFO event is not its physical trace, but its impact on society at the level of myth. In this sense, he sees the UFO working through subcultures throughout the world and even identifies this as a new form of religion.

"You will find people in remote towns in California who have literally dropped out of city life (where they had held responsible positions and enjoyed good salaries) because they had received messages from space instructing them to do so. They would be regarded as perfectly square if it were not for the fact that their lives have been changed by what they consider to be genuine extraterrestrial communication. One such man left Los Angeles with his family after a message he believes came from Jupiter instructed him to find an isolated spot and live in semiretirement, 'providing a center of peace in the world of intense turmoil that was to come.' We are not here dealing with escapism—we are dealing with the next form of religion."[7]

The ensuing pages outline the lived realities of the practitioners of this new spiritual reorientation. While billionaires clamor to acquire UFO data to create new super technologies and governments carefully manage the public perception of UFOs through new programs affiliated with major universities, witnesses and experiencers quietly continue to live the missions that they feel are uniquely theirs.

1

THE SPACE PSYCHOLOGIST

Nothing distinguishes the ancient from the modern man so much as the former's absorption in a cosmic experience scarcely known to later periods. . . . Men as a species completed their development thousands of years ago; but mankind as a species is just beginning his. . . . In technology, a physis is being organized through which mankind's contact with the cosmos takes a new and different form from that which it had in nations and families.

—WALTER BENJAMIN, "TO THE PLANETARIUM"

LMP Boy, that sure is weird music.
CMP We're going to have to find out about that. Nobody will believe us.
LMP Yes. It's a whistling, you know, like an outer-space-type thing. . . .
LMP I don't know. But I'll tell you, that eerie music is what's bothering me. You know that—
CMP God damn, I heard it, too.
LMP You know, that was funny. That's just like

something from outer space, really. Who's
going to believe it?

CMP   Nobody. Shall we tell them about it?

LMP   I don't know. We ought to think about it
some.

—DECLASSIFIED TRANSCRIPT OF APOLLO 10 MISSION

"It's a one-way ticket," Tyler D. said. He was lounging in
the morning sunshine. The bright light reflected off his avi-
ator glasses.

I watched the sunbeams dance off his sunglasses while
he told me about the imminent human exploration of Mars.
We were in Palo Alto for a meeting with Drs. Garry Nolan
and Jacques Vallée, two scientists with whom we worked on
the topic of UFOs. SpaceX's rocket had just exploded. Tyler's
phone was in a constant flurry of notifications as astronauts
and aerospace engineers asked him for advice. He reached
for the phone and turned it off.

"Make sure you tell your kids," he said, in reference to
the Mars mission. "They're at the prime age for targeted recruitment."

My oldest child was in the third grade.

I considered his words. Tyler's affiliations with space
industry heavyweights like NASA, the aerospace industry, SpaceX, the Department of Defense, and the US Air
Force, among others, provided him with access to credible
information about marketing space programs and jobs to
youth. His job as a mission controller at Cape Canaveral was
one of the longest held by one individual. He commanded

respect both inside and outside the industry. *Eight-year-old children?* I thought. Whoever planned this campaign was on a long timeline.

I knew that Tyler told me certain information because he had great affection for my children. Throughout the several years we worked together, he often told me things that he thought would benefit me as a mother.

One of my favorite activities was to walk with my children at dusk. We would walk through our neighborhood and observe the wildlife in the American South—raccoons, possums, and sometimes a stray cat or coyote would dart by. We'd talk to neighbors as the darkness of night slowly replaced the yellow brightness of day.

When Tyler warned me about the recruitment plan to which he had been privy I didn't ask him to explain its details, because, as with all things he said to me, I had no way to verify the information. His job status prevented him from being completely transparent. I didn't want my kids to aspire to go to Mars, however. At this point in human history, it was obvious that it would be a one-way ticket, just as he said.

I returned home from Palo Alto. During the dusk walk, I took the opportunity to talk to my kids about what I had learned.

"So, you know that if you become an astronaut and sign on to go to Mars, you will not come back? Right?" It was early evening and about midway through our walk when I posited the question to my eldest daughter, the head of the pack. If she agreed, the younger ones would follow her lead.

"Okay!" she chirped.

My younger kids were probably confused, or they didn't

care, but at the time they nodded in agreement. They enjoyed the walks as much as I did, and they liked Mr. Tyler and his stories. He used to tell them all about flying jet airplanes and launching rockets in Florida, and they especially laughed hysterically at his stories about the Vomit Comet.

The Vomit Comet is a special airplane that helps astronauts acclimate to zero-gravity environments. It climbs to a very high elevation and then drops into a free fall. During the period in which the plane drops, the astronauts-in-training float in the air, weightless, preparing their bodies and minds for what they will feel when they are in space. The Vomit Comet also makes people very sick. Human bodies, unsurprisingly, resist being plunged toward Earth at high speeds while they float around in a high-tech metal tube. Tyler holds a record for being one of the most ill of all the people who have flown on the Vomit Comet. My kids screamed with laughter when he described being carried off the plane, unable to walk from retching. He spent that day in the hospital. He offered, several times, to get me a spot on the Vomit Comet, but I declined. Currently, nonastronauts can purchase the pleasure of this experience through a company called Zero Gravity Corporation.

Being weightless, I learned, was the least traumatic experience astronauts face while traveling in space. Approximately six hundred astronauts have left Earth's atmosphere and, from this new vantage point, have gazed back at their home planet. No other group of people in human history have had this view. This *literal shift in worldview* is often accompanied by shock, awe, dread, and sometimes trauma and personal transformation. To see Earth as a blue globe suspended in a black backdrop of what appears to be infinite space in every direction engenders a lot of different emotions. Two of the most common emotions appear to be entirely new to human consciousness, or so unfamiliar that astronauts have a hard time finding words to describe them. Physicist Rosalyn Yalow noted, "New truths become evident when new tools become available." Technological tools like rockets, space capsules, rovers, and technologies that extend human senses to the surface of Mars and to places that are far away from Earth bring about new experiences, new truths, and new mental states.

This novel consciousness, which astronauts find difficult to describe, requires a new vocabulary or requires *the remembrance* of a lost vocabulary. Some of the terms that have been used to describe these new mental states are found in the history of religions. When astronaut Edgar Mitchell saw Earth from his tiny capsule floating through space, his mental state altered so much it changed his life and its direction. He returned to Earth determined to find an explanation for his palpably electrifying experience. His search was not easy, but he finally found that the only thing that came close to a description was the ecstatic experience illustrated in Hindu and Buddhist sacred texts called "samadhi," which is the feeling in body and mind of being completely connected with all that is, that is, with all of reality.

Since the nineteenth century, scholars of religion have worked out vocabularies to describe rare and sublime states that people who experience them ironically describe as indescribable. The sacred text of Daoism famously begins with this paradox: "The Dao that can be told is not the eternal

Dao." Early twentieth-century German scholar of religion Rudolf Otto called these experiences "numinous." The numinous is the feeling of being in the presence of awesome power, which is simultaneously mysterious, dreadful, fascinating, and difficult to describe. A common assumption is that religious or spiritual experiences are uplifting and filled with joy. Data from the archives of religious studies reveal a more complicated story: most people are completely unhinged by their forays into spiritual experiences. As the stories of the prophets of the Hebrew Bible illustrate, if God knocks in the middle of the night, prophets jump ship. They run the other way, and sometimes, such as in the prophet Jonah's case, literally. However, the stories also reveal that one cannot escape a force like God.

The incongruity of what one *expects* from the experience of being in space compared to what *is experienced* was richly illustrated by none other than the most beloved starship captain—Captain Kirk of the famous television series *Star Trek,* otherwise known as actor William Shatner. Shatner, ninety years old at the time, had never been to space, so space entrepreneur Jeff Bezos, owner of Blue Origin, invited him to fly to space in the company's space capsule in October 2021. Shatner's experience was filled with wonder *and* trauma.

"I was crying," Shatner said. "I didn't know what I was crying about. I had to go off some place and sit down and think, what's the matter with me? And I realized I was in grief. . . . It was the death that I saw in space and the life-force that I saw coming from the planet—the blue, the beige and the white. And I realized one was death and the other was life."[1]

Shatner expected to be elated, but he was, instead, reduced to tears. His words illustrate feelings of dread, fear, and respect, as he describes space as a funeral and Earth as life. Shatner had a classic brush with the numinous. How are we, the recipients of a fellow nonastronaut's testimony about the new frontier, supposed to process this frightful information? As fate would have it, this question is answered by none other than a scientist whose job was forged within the rapid pace of the space and aeronautics industry. Iya Whiteley is a British space psychologist, born in Latvia and whose mission is to support pilots and astronauts as they enter these extreme environments. Her task is to design tools and training for happy and efficient living and working in Earth's orbit, on the Moon, and on a return mission to Mars. Working out what the crew may face on missions beyond our Earth's orbit, Iya developed the Psy-Matrix, where over thirty-six groups of challenges are systematically assessed, which include how to acclimate to new mental states and to the shock of a new consciousness.[2]

FIRST CONTACT WITH IYA

Dr. Iya Whiteley contacted me through a series of emails in 2020. The subject line of the emails caught my attention right away: "Space Psychologist—researcher at a university in London. Developing communication means with unknown phenomena." *What?! Who was this?!* I thought as I quickly searched her name on the internet. I read her university biography: Dr. Iya Whiteley, a space psychologist exploring the human mind to develop our abilities and to realize our potential while we explore outer space. I thought it was bold and even brave for an established space scientist and academic to reach out to me in her own name about a means of communication with unknown phenomena. The unknown phenomena I had been known to research were UFOs. *What's the catch?* I thought. Perhaps there was none, but years of doing research into UFOs and the beliefs of scientists—most of who want to remain anonymous regarding the topic—had accustomed me to preserve, or at least expect, the anonymity of scientific UFO researchers. I responded enthusiastically to her first email, and then I didn't hear from her for weeks. I thought she had reconsidered reaching out. Then one day I received another note. I opened it to find that she had been in South America in February and March of 2020. "I was there doing research into our common interest," she later said.

The COVID-19 pandemic had caused the shutdown of the borders in the countries in which she was traveling, and she was trying to get back to England, where she lived and worked. Each subsequent email arrived from a different country. She was flying from country to country with borders closing behind her one by one with no knowledge of when or if the borders would open again. Her situation, which I observed with horror through my computer in the safe environment of my home, was extreme. She later explained that relative to many experiences from her life, hopping from country to country as the pandemic was spreading was not so difficult.

"I'm a pilot; I jump from flying airplanes (I am a champion skydiver); I scuba dive and research in extreme environments, so I can understand what goes through the minds of people working and making split-second decisions. I support the needs of people in these environments, and I need to have had these experiences myself so I can best help them," she said.

Iya studied psychology and computer science, the novel field of study called cognitive engineering, putting together complex information onto electronic displays for modern aircrafts. Among her other tasks using voice-analysis technology that she coinvented is to provide early detection of fatigue and to monitor the well-being of astronauts in extreme environments.

She explained that as astronauts would get farther and farther from the Earth, they would form their own rules, beliefs, and behaviors and, at times without any discussion, would form an understanding of what is acceptable and what is not acceptable. These rules and behaviors could drastically differ from those of the society they left behind. Mission control and people on the ground might find these new rules and behaviors shocking and unacceptable, but given the surrounding circumstances, it would be natural to transition to these new rules.

It was through Iya that I learned about the psychology of space travel and new forms of consciousness that appear to develop within these new environments. Documented psychological states that are specific to space travel include the Overview Effect, which has received the most publicity, and the less glamorous state described by William Shatner, which appears to be an encounter with the numinous.

The Overview Effect was described by space theorist and author Frank White in the 1980s. At that time there were enough astronauts who reported similar feelings about being in space and seeing Earth from space to identify an initial pattern. White observed, "The Overview Effect is the experience of seeing the Earth from a distance, especially from orbit or the Moon, and realizing the inherent unity and oneness of everything on the planet. The Effect represents a shift in perception wherein the viewer moves from identification with parts of the Earth to identification with the whole system."[3] Astronaut Russell Schweickart described his experience as if he were part of Earth as a type of sensing instrument: "When you go around the Earth in an hour and a half, you begin to recognize that your identity is with that whole thing. And that makes a change. . . . [I]t comes through to you so powerfully that you're the sensing element for man."[4]

After White described the effect, he and public intellectuals like Carl Sagan thought that the testimonies of astronauts about the effect, as well as the photographs taken from the Moon of the Earth, might replicate in a small way the same experience for people on Earth. White and others conjectured that if people felt this effect they might identify with their planet, like the astronauts did, and choose to take care of it and maybe even each other. This hopeful interpretation has continued to inspire contemporary movements and organizations, such as the Overview Institute, which funds educational programs about the positive effects of space travel as well as the creation of immersive virtual environments intended to replicate the effect. The institute hopes that it can bring this shift in consciousness, which so far has only been identified in some astronauts, to "Earth-bound millions."[5] Immersive environments have not been able to accurately replicate the effect, however. Many astronauts said that the feeling was visceral and that "photographs do not accurately convey the actual experience."[6]

A more complicated mental state that can afflict astronauts is the feeling Iya described as noncomforming and which increases the farther away they travel from Earth in their space capsules. Again, this may appear to us who remain on Earth as irrational, but Iya noted it was completely acceptable given the circumstances the crew might experience. The training astronauts undergo is famously rigorous and intense and ideally would include situations wherein crew may see their mates go through changes in their belief systems. Additionally, astronauts are chosen because they fit specific personality profiles. Along with stringent physical and mental training, they also take a barrage of personality tests. Scientist-psychologists like Iya are trained to identify candidates who can flourish in extreme environments. Given these circumstances, it is not surprising that astronauts are impeccable at self-control, especially with respect to their emotions. Feelings like dread, fear, and panic would go undetected by their team, and even by themselves. Additionally, space equipment, including capsules and habitats, are worth billions of dollars, so a fatigued or irrational astronaut who might act unpredictably is a very real concern for space institutions. The consequences of this (so far) unnamed mental state are very real and potentially dangerous. In the United States Space Station, Skylab

4, the astronauts on board at one point just stopped working. They reported that they were unable to maintain their scheduled tests and duties as they were so confused by the new "baffling, fascinating, unprecedented experiences" of floating around in space.[7]

Iya led the European Space Agency study that systematically defined how best to prepare, monitor, and prevent psychological issues that arise during exploration missions to the Moon and Mars. She defined technologies and techniques to address the identified psychological needs of the astronauts in order to sustain their mental health and stamina. In extreme environments and exploration missions, prevention is key. With a colleague, she developed technology to detect what astronauts themselves and mission control are unable to detect, such as onset of fatigue and the effects of extended sleep deprivation that can play tricks on the mind and perception. These devices decipher hints of fatigue in the voices of astronauts. Safety is the priority, and identifying changes in the crew that may compromise safety and put a mission in jeopardy is vital. The aim is to prevent any situation that could cost crews' lives and endanger very expensive equipment. Iya led projects to develop EPSILON (Embedded Psychological Support Integrated for LONg-duration missions), a tool set for exploration expeditions to the Moon and Mars, and she designed tools to help crews resolve challenges that emerge in new alien environments, particularly those where there is no live communication with Earth. Iya's work contributed to a change in the culture of pilots reporting automation anomalies and is instrumental in identifying many forms of consciousness that are produced in space environments. She is our best interpreter of the global shift in perspective, which had been mere thoughts and speculations in the minds of philosophers and futurists who saw these developments years and years before she was born.

THE TWENTY-FIRST-CENTURY INTERFACE WITH HYPEROBJECTS: MIND SHIFT

In 1917, the German-Jewish intellectual Walter Benjamin wrote a short essay on the consequences for humanity of a *shift in perspective* toward celestial objects. He wrote that the sight of celestial objects, like the billions of stars in the Milky Way, had always occurred from the perspective of a community, like a tribe or a family. He wrote that now the sight of the "heavens" would become increasingly singular as human beings increase their abilities to see celestial objects through technologies like telescopes. In the brief two-page essay, "To the Planetarium," Benjamin made several predictions and observations. First, he mourned the loss of a communal experience of seeing the stars with family and friends. This, he said, had been a shared ecstatic experience. He predicted that technology would bring humanity a new view, one that never existed before. In that sense, he described technology as a *physis,* which is something organic, bound to happen, and in development. Physis describes an inevitable process, like the development of an apple seed into an apple. Benjamin identified this historic shift, but as all things that uncannily forecast a future reality, it wasn't completely right. As astronauts leave Earth and view space, many do experience ecstasy, and people on Earth have a taste of it too. It is still a communal experience, but it is also something that Benjamin couldn't have predicted. It is an interface with the truly alien.[8]

Astronauts who leave Earth often describe something like Otto's idea of the numinous. These emotions include fear, trembling, and respect. The consciousness of space travel is so new that researchers have just begun to make headway into understanding what is happening to space-farers and what it could possibly mean for billions of earth-bound people. What does it mean that many astronauts describe experiences that resemble those described by mystics of past religious and spiritual traditions?

Anthropologist Deana Weibel analyzes the reports of astronauts' experiences in space and how they impact their cosmologies or views of the universe. She addresses the Overview Effect but also identifies another state, which she coined the Ultraview Effect. The Ultraview Effect incorporates the more perplexing and disturbing aspects of these new experiences. She explores the ways in which encountering the Earth and other celestial objects in ways never before experienced by human beings has influenced some astronauts' cosmological understandings.

Weibel recognized that there was considerable overlap between astronauts' descriptions and those described by scholar Timothy Morton with respect to "hyperobjects." Morton wrote that hyperobjects are objects that exist yet are *almost* unfathomable to comprehend. They include objects found in other dimensions, such as Platonic solids, but also objects that are so large that they are a shock to human comprehension:

There exists a reality to certain huge objects or systems that is separate from humanity's ability to perceive them. While human beings throughout the ages have had a slow but increasing awareness of large objects (like the globe or the ocean, for example), Morton specifically used hyperobject to refer to "massively distributed entities that can be thought or computered, but not directly touched or seen," meaning our main awareness of them is achieved through the use of technology.[9]

Weibel credits Morton for recognizing that "human 'contact' with these objects is transformative in a very disruptive way." She notes, "Hyperobjects are normally phased, meaning we only see parts of them at any given time, so they seem to come and go. In this view, the reality of a thing exists apart from our piecemeal impressions of the reality of things, and at this point in time we are starting, slowly, to comprehend them in their entirety."[10]

The cognition of hyperobjects through technology— both at the micro level enabled by the use of computers, which can model objects in other dimensions, and at the macro level with the use of telescopes and space capsules to view massive objects in space, which are encountered within the seemingly infinite substrate of space—constitutes the historic moment in which we live now. "This is the historical moment at which hyperobjects become visible by humans. This visibility changes everything."[11] Although Benjamin did not include hyperobjects—objects which are almost incomprehensible to human cognition—within his description of this shift, he certainly captured the spirit of the epoch just as it began. Significantly, Plato identified hyperobjects with the use of math. Math, and the technologies and computer languages that create them, is the bridge to this new shift in perspective.

Morton characterizes the emotions aroused by encountering these objects as pain and disgust. Weibel's analysis reveals an experience more in line with Otto's idea of the numinous. She notes, "Our familiar illusions are replaced with a frightening perception of something truly alien." This new sight, in other words, initiates a shift in worldview. This consciousness of what is truly "alien" reorients those who encounter it. Russell Schweickart described himself as a literal instrument, a "sensing element for man." Edgar Mitchell felt a "palpable" experience of divinity and connection in space that led to a life-long exploration of the noetic transmission of knowledge.[12] The new consciousness, powerfully felt and embodied by Schweickart and Mitchell, suggests that the human body and mind, confronted with hyperobjects in space, undergo a process of reception of consciousness that they are compelled to transmit to others. Researchers who study the psychological states of astronauts observe that, just as Otto remarked about the encounter with the numinous, "awe can transform people and reorient their lives, goals, and values. Given the stability of personality and values . . . awe-inducing events may be one of the fastest and most powerful methods of personal change and growth."[13]

Among those who experienced these alien mental states, some were struck with a feeling that extraterrestrial life is inevitable. Weibel's sensitive elaboration of an Apollo astronaut's experience illustrates this shift in worldview:

> Looking at the universe out there from my vantage point, I began to realize that we don't know crap about anything, we really don't. . . . [A]t some points in my orbit around the moon, I was sheltered from both the earth and the sun, so I was in complete darkness. And all of a sudden, the star patterns out there became something that I was not ready for. . . . So many stars I couldn't see one. Just a sheet of light. I don't know whether you'd call it spiritual or not, but when I saw the starfield out there in a way that nobody else has ever seen . . . I had some pretty profound thoughts. . . . We are not unique in the universe. When I came back from my flight, we were all totally exhausted. . . . I'd sit in my living room and all these thoughts would come flowing through, so I began writing them down. . . . They flowed from my mind through a pen onto a piece of paper. It was like I was being guided by something.[14]

As with people who have had UFO experiences, Zack, a pseudonym, reviewed and then revised his own religious tradition, which was Protestant. What he had thought of as angels before, he now understood as cosmic entities. This interpretative move is called the sacred text–UFO hermeneutic and is common among religious UFO experiencers.

After the shock of either seeing a UFO or having an experience that opens one to the possibility that extraterrestrial life exists, a person from a religious background will often review their tradition and identify contact events between people and divinities as extraterrestrial. Even atheists and agnostics undergo a similar process. After his trip to space, William Shatner, who is not religious, shared his belief that we are not alone:

> "It's impossible for [this] to be the only world," Shatner explained. "There are other intelligent entities out there, probably since life is so ardent. There's such passion in life that . . . it's everywhere. . . . And everything in life has a passion to live. So, you think that's only on this little rocky planet?"[15]

In the population of people who are not astronauts, these experiences often produce two data sets.[16] Academics and ufologists who hear the testimonies of people who have extreme experiences, such as being a witness to a UFO event, relate that there were often two types of reports by the very people who reported. "People tended to report different things depending on to whom they were speaking." People often report empirical evidence—things seen and heard—to authorities and academics, and then report what they experienced subjectively to their families. They do this because of the fear of being ridiculed, which is very real. When the astronauts heard what they called eerie space music on the Apollo 10 mission, they decided not to report it, as they said, "Who's going to believe it?" They thought it was absurd. Space-type music in space! This fear of ridicule impacts the data needed to assess space environments.

What's unique and potentially innovative about studies on astronauts is the sheer amount of data that astronauts provide and the techniques used to extract it. Astronauts are data mines for the aerospace industry, so all information, from physiological data to emotional and psychological data, is expected from them and extracted by experts.

A psychologist with specializations like Iya's is aware when people are hiding information. Iya knows that astronauts are rational, so if they expose a newfound belief in alien life, she receives it as data. This neutral observation, apparently so simple, is, in actuality, a radical innovation in method with transformative potential. Most academics, if they do study the topic of UFOs, couch reports of beliefs in extraterrestrial life with references to the credibility of the person who reports the event. In Weibel's assessment of Zack's newfound worldview, she writes that he is "a rational person, a successful author and businessman, but his unconventional religious beliefs were absolutely influenced by his time in space, which he said changed his idea of infinity and his whole outlook." The unconventional religious belief is his idea that "we are not unique in the universe." Weibel is not alone in her citation of the credibility of the witness; I have done this with all my writings about the topic of UFOs. It is a natural reaction to a culture of silence and ridicule. With respect to the culture of ridicule, the potential benefit of Iya's method for the culture that surrounds UFOs should not be underestimated. If applied, it will be revolutionary.

SHIFTING THE CULTURE OF SILENCE: FROM AVIATION TO UFOS

Iya speaks with an Eastern European–English-inflected accent. Her intelligence is striking and could potentially intimidate anyone, yet she is disarmingly kind and down-to-earth. No doubt this combination of traits has inspired the confidence of thousands of pilots and many astronauts.

"I worked with pilots during my PhD and adapted a method I call iViewExpert," she said. "It is intended to bring preverbal memory to the surface of consciousness. There is preverbal knowing and professional intuition that experts are unaware they know or can share. They know what to do, but filter it out depending on the audience. Why do they do it? They ignore sharing the most precious intuition that, as in the case of a surgeon, if passed on to another surgeon can save someone's life. That is the question that my method helps to fix.

"The interesting aspect here is that most experts do not even realize or are not conscious of the fact that they carry expert knowledge. They do not know how to share it or they think they already do share their expertise, but apparently, not fully. This is exactly where the precious jewels of knowledge hide and must be passed on to help us thrive as a society."

I had watched Iya speak at a conference of aerospace experts. The topic was aviation safety and optimization. I noticed that Iya's contributions were always creative and novel. She mentioned that instead of designing cockpits according to engineering logic, engineers should take into consideration "pilot logic," as the aircraft would be flown by pilots, not engineers. Pilots should dictate the design. Luckily, now part of the design process are human-factors experts, like Iya, who read pilots' minds in order to make the flying process seamless for them. "This is how I received the United States Air Force Research Laboratory award and was able to disseminate my research in the United States, at the Wright-Patterson Air Force Base, Boeing, and NASA."

The idea is for the pilot to feel the aircraft and think it is reading the pilot's mind and only gives the absolute bare-minimum information to assist in making prompt and accurate decisions. The challenge for human-factors experts is that truly talented pilots "fly by the seat of their pants" and are not talkative about how they do it. Pilots get thrown hundreds of bits of information at them in a split second, choose the right ones, and store the rest for later to be recalled, and they make it look easy maneuvering these beastly machines, as if they are toys. If, indeed, pilots look like they are enjoying flying and not making any mistakes, this is when Iya's job is done well. She also mentioned that all information needs to be intuitive and natural to observe. For example, she said that safety notifications should be audial and tonal so that if pilots or astronauts hear disharmony they will immediately be alerted to an issue. Her research methods were so successful that they eventually permeated the aviation industry.

"I started my research into the misinterpretation of information, and I read reports of aviation accidents and problems; sometimes they'd come in every week," Iya said.

"The era of 'the safety culture and no blame/no shame

reporting' was just beginning at the time and a new type of technology was introduced into aviation. We went from analogue cockpits (clocklike instruments) to computer screens (glass cockpits). I developed coherent principles for information presentation on aircraft displays to prevent errors. This was *only possible* due to the bravery of pilots who began to report what they saw, or their confusion about things. Slowly pilots began to record incidents because they were not being punished or fired, and there were comprehensive investigations of aerial accidents."

Iya described the culture of silence that permeated the vast industries of aviation. I'd heard about this socially sanctioned industry practice from pilots, one astronaut, and Tyler, who, like Iya, worked directly with astronauts. I wrote about it as a *Fight Club* environment, in reference to the novel of the same name by Chuck Palahniuk, in which a culture of men is bound by a strict rule of silence. Until very recently, as Iya indicated, pilots were discouraged from reporting abnormalities or things that suggested they were possibly confused by data presented on screens or in their environment. UFOs were strictly off-limits with respect to being reported. The culture of "no reporting" any abnormalities led to accidents and the deaths of thousands of people. Iya was on the edge of the new culture of accepting all reports, even of things unknown.

Iya shared a report on aviation safety statistics. I could see that the number of aviation-related fatalities decreased significantly and indeed followed the timeline of the cultural shift that Iya described. The shift included, among other things, a decentralization of information. Instead of a hierarchy of reports, teams worked together to address problems.

"For the first time, the investigation team included all types of experts, from aviation and airline policy groups, to management, aircraft repair mechanics, airport staff, and cabin crew. Also, they included representatives from trade unions, and data scientists. The problems were no longer just recorded as 'pilot error.'

"A lot of the errors were due to pilots being put under extreme pressure from management to save fuel. For example, they were punished for flying extra circuits around the airport. They did this because they were unsure of the state of the aircraft or the runway. But they were pressured not to do this, to save fuel. Over a long period of time and due to combinations of conflicting types of pressure, it appears that some pilots committed suicide due to being disrespected by the company and their colleagues or due to family pressure."

Iya's work helped shift the culture. Her analysis of the data and her interviews with multiple players within the aviation industry revealed that the problems that caused fatal accidents were the same in almost all instances. The whole industry recognized the problem of needing to be open, without shame or blame, about sharing any type of pilot confusion, incidence, and multidimensional accident analysis.

"All of these types of pressures began to dissolve," she said.

"The culture of safe reporting started to take hold as an online worldwide database confirmed that the misinterpretation of information and management-related pressures were widespread and similar in nature! I was one of many scientists able to work through the data and distill the common threads, and then I started to address them."

The timeline for the shift in culture was a generation.

"This cultural change within the industry took twenty to twenty-five years, which is the length of one professional life," Iya said. She also noted that as older professionals leave, the new generation sees that it is okay to report errors. "They do not have the experiences of seeing colleagues being punished for preventing incidences and accidents. Hence, the new generation persists with a 'new' culture of safety reporting. Of course, for the new generation, it is not 'new.' It is now a very much established reporting culture.

"I see the need for the same steps to take place to develop the UFO safety reporting culture," she said. "I have studied pilots and astronauts. They are different populations. With pilots it is easy for me to identify what is being unsaid. With astronauts, they are now trained for public speaking and social media interaction so well, I often do not see what is unsaid. There is a wall."

There was a pause in our conversation, and then she added, "And I'm pretty good at reading people."

After this conversation I thought about her last words. I felt that I knew very well about the wall she identified. It is the reason why Tyler D. is a pseudonymous name and continues to be for the foreseeable future. It is the reason that very public people with affiliations like Tyler's always give away some information to the public but hold back, citing their "clearances." I heard that astronauts had to sign nondisclosure agreements. I once asked Tyler why this was the case. The answer was obvious to him, and he knew it should be to me, too, but I asked anyway.

"Because they see shit in space," he said, as a matter of fact.

I had asked him this question in 2018, and between then and now, things have changed completely. Now that other countries are in space, not just Russia and the United States, whatever it is that may have been hidden from the public will now be inevitably visible. The cultural shift is no longer an option.

Iya proposes a way forward. In collaboration we discussed the two categories of reports that overlap but are also distinct. I shared my research data and contacts. I explained that there appeared to be a sphere of influence when sightings were reported. One data set from Australia clearly revealed that people had reported experiences with beings that they associated with crafts but had not seen crafts themselves. Independent reports, verified by local police stations, revealed that multiple witnesses from the same location, who did not know each other, reported crafts during the same time period that other people saw beings or had strange dreams, but did not see crafts. Therefore, in many instances there is a sphere of influence that impacts people who have not seen a craft but are in the vicinity of where crafts have been sighted. I introduced Iya to naval personnel who had been in the vicinity of the UFOs that had been reported by air force pilots and on radar. Although these personnel did not see actual crafts, they experienced vivid dreams and had contact with beings that they believed were associated with the crafts.

If the matter was just one of reporting an unknown craft in the sky, the cultural shift would be less complicated. The fact that people are seeing and experiencing things that are completely out of the ordinary and are the topic of cultural stigmatization requires a creative strategy to move forward.

"There are brave men and women who set the precedent in terms of reporting UFOs, yet if there are no further additional measures of positive reinforcement introduced, it would take another professional generation, approximately twenty-five years of professional life, to change the current climate and culture to one of openness and acceptance. If this has to be done in two professional generations, one being for UFOs and one for intelligent-beings contact—we are looking at forty-five to fifty years. This would be too long for people who already have been dealing with the consequences of contact, such as loss of professional standing, loss of income, loss of families, and even more drastic: children losing parents and children experiencing contact without the acceptance and support of others.

"To put this into perspective, if people do fall into PTSD [post-traumatic stress disorder] or depression, as a result of not being accepted, or if their professional experience as trained observers is questioned, the consequences are devastating. . . . There are further problems for the younger generation and our society if their parents are struggling with depression."

"Diana," she said. "Time is what we do not have to assist those who are already going through these life-changing experiences now."

I listened to the urgency in Iya's voice. Just after our conversation I felt motivated to introduce her to people involved in the task force called the Human Factors UAP (Unidentified Aerial Phenomena) Committee organized by an air force pilot who had been making news about UFOs in United States airspace. I was reassured to know that Iya, who has made such a necessary improvement to safety within the culture of aviation, was now going to attempt to do the same for UFO reports and those who make them. The generational shift that Iya had been instrumental in achieving is gaining momentum. Perhaps there will come a day when the scientists who study UFOs will not need to call this research "their hobby." It turns out that Iya's "hobby research" is even more interesting than her noteworthy accomplishments in aeronautics and aviation. It also sheds light on aspects of UFO events that are not commonly emphasized. These include nonordinary mental states that suggest a form of extended cognition to an organic information network.

TECHNOLOGY AND AI

A Language Bridge Back to Contact

And, stop asking the question, "Are we alone?" Of
course we're not! Everything in the universe is alive
and full of knowledge.

—TYSON YUNKAPORTA, *SAND TALK*

It was a beautiful day—the sun shone bright, and the air glit-
tered with a mixture of ocean spray and sea salt. My partner
and I sat on a dock on the ocean along the North Carolina
coast. As I dodged cold droplets from breaking waves, I told
him about my discovery of the Order of the Dolphin, which
was the name of a small group of scientists from the 1960s
and '70s who tried to find a way to contact nonhuman intelligent life. They were pragmatic enough to begin their
research on terrestrial nonhuman intelligence—dolphins.
This is also why they chose the dolphin as the totemic name
of their group. They kept their work secret, as they were
all well-known scientists; among them was Carl Sagan. As
I spoke, a very large gray-blue dolphin breached about ten
feet from where we sat. We both immediately jumped from

our seats in fright. Its tall dorsal fin conjured scenes in our minds from the movie *Jaws*. We laughed when we realized that we both thought that the huge animal was a shark! It splashed back into the water and swam away.

I had come across references to the Order of the Dolphin at the Vatican Observatory. The observatory sits on top of the volcanic grounds of Castel Gandolfo, Italy, and on the rim of a deep sky-blue lake. Its beauty and relative proximity to the Vatican established this center as the official papal summer residence. The director of the observatory is Brother Guy Consolmagno, an astronomer, physicist, and monk of the Catholic Church. He had told me that all of the Vatican's space-related material, which has included original copies of sixteenth-century astronomer Johannes Kepler's cosmologies and a large meteorite collection, is shipped to the observatory's archive. It is a repository of Western civilization's most innovative thoughts on space, space travel, and humanity's place within the universe.

As I looked over the old books in the small, solitary archive, I discovered several references to the work of the Order of the Dolphin. When I returned home, I learned more. The scientists made some salient points about Western academic's methods and attempts to establish contact with nonhumans in our proximate environment. These mostly consist of trying to teach animals human language, instead of attempting to learn theirs. There are estimated to be many millions of species of animals on Earth, yet Western scientists are only aware of approximately 1.5 million. As Sagan wrote, "It is of interest to note that while some dolphins are reported to have learned English—up to fifty words used in correct context—no human being has been reported to have learned dolphinese."

The secrecy of the order, which I had discussed with my partner, stayed in my thoughts. Why would attempts to make meaningful contact with beings—animal, plant, or otherwise—cause scholars to resort to secrecy about their efforts? What was so threatening? I returned to my reflections on some scientists' reference to their UFO research as a *hobby*. Tyler D., who also engages in innovative work in the field, insists that this work has nothing to do with his "day job," and that it is just a hobby. Similarly, Iya Whiteley's passion, of which her aerospace cognitive-engineering background laid the groundwork, is the creation of a "nation-independent" global and cosmic language. As she explained to me, it has nothing to do with her work at the university. One clear pattern that unites these three scientists is their innovation, and extreme innovation pushes one to the edge of socially sanctioned reality. Maybe one reason why people like Iya and Jacques disassociate their hobbies from their daytime jobs is because their work creates new fields of inquiry and doesn't reaffirm old ones.

Iya's current research reverses the problem that Sagan identified. He noted that people haven't learned the language of animals and that the quest to contact them has been one-sided. Researchers attempt to teach animals our language but have not been able to learn theirs. Iya's project reverses the trend by focusing on the language of other species. By doing this, she has identified the contours of an Earth language. Most importantly, she believes she is taking initial steps to develop a means of connection with nonhuman intelligent species.

THE NEWBORN GLOBAL LANGUAGE PROJECT

Iya helped initiate a generational shift in aviation that led to safer plane flights for everyone. For her, this was a precursor to her real work. Her real work is the identification of what she terms a cosmic and global language. Her intention is no less than the facilitation of a new generation of people who are receptive to and able to be in connection with the intelligences that surround all of us, globally and in the natural world.

Iya's program starts at the most formative time in the life of a human being, which is the first six months of life. It operates at the level of neural networks as it gently introduces newborns to a cosmic perceptual network—human and nonhuman. Iya believes that this network, which is discussed in many experiencers' reports, predates the internet and connects animals, plants, insects, and otherworlds. Her goal is to prepare the new generation, on a cognitive level, for the proliferation of a universal and nation-independent language.

Iya used intuition as a guide as she created technologies to support pilots and contributed to the global safety culture of aviation. She was rewarded with spectacular success and recognition. Intuition guided her to identify and create the technologies that are now used by pilots and astronauts. The genesis for her Earth language program was born through her desire to share her own interests with her child.

"The story of this discovery goes back to the birth of our baby. I wanted to share the wonders from our Earth's nature, the art, and amazing inventions with my newborn, but all I could find in bookshops were simplistic pictures of cats and shadows and chessboards. I was surprised that we have been to the Moon and back, built the Large Hadron Collider to collide the smallest particles, and yet to our precious babies we still show simplistic and not even realistic views of the world when they arrive Earth-side."

I smiled as I listened to Iya describe her work. Her words are sprinkled with references to Earth and space and reveal a mind that exists simultaneously in multiple worlds— terrestrial, cosmic, transcendent.

"I thought," she said, "that I've designed sophisticated modern digital aircraft displays specifically fitted for the rapid cognitive processes of pilots. I have won awards and have been recognized by the Air Force Office of Scientific Research and have been asked to present the processes and concept designs at the Air Force Research Laboratory at the Wright-Patterson Air Force Base, Dayton, Ohio, to Boeing and to NASA. Surely, I can follow the same design process for newborn babies.

"Just as I deciphered the cognitive needs of pilots, I set out to understand the perceptual principles by which babies would be engaged. I distilled design principles and selected images to fit newborn babies' visual perception and cognitive processing. Within a few weeks, I had a set of images based on the realistic representation of the world around us. My baby was mesmerized, and so were the babies of my friends. Babies would study images from a few seconds on day one to several minutes in a week and to hours in a few months, increasing their concentation tremendously."

"How do you choose the images, and what are they?" I asked.

"I experience the Earth consciousness as a pattern that is manifesting repeatedly through vibrations in sounds and visual forms in nature, trying to reach out to us," she said.

"I believe, throughout the generations, many cultures perceived it, but we in the Western society have yet to interpret it. We can, through the use of technology, begin to decipher some elements of it in our generation. The interpretation of these ancient Earth sounds and patterns is exactly what I am setting out to do. This is a global and cosmic language."

She shared some of the images and audio files with me. She graphed the sounds of certain insects and animal species into geometric patterns. These are the graphemes to be shared with infants. Each grapheme is part of the language. It is accompanied by the sounds and this helps identify underlying patterns.

"I propose a radically different approach to gain an understanding of the meaning behind these patterns. We can do this in two generations. Our generation will create the alphabet, and the new generation will learn the language from birth. In known human history, we have not acquired this Earth language as something independent of one specific culture yet."

TECHNOLOGY: HOW THE LANGUAGE BRIDGE WORKS

Iya is one of a group of scientists and scholars who are on the verge of contact and, in her case, connection with nonhuman intelligent species. Although these scientists hail from different fields, such as anthropology, neuroscience, or aeronautics, a common pattern that unites their efforts is the use of technology. Perhaps the most famous among this group is biologist Roger Payne, who, in the 1960s, used the then-new technology of hydrophones (underwater microphones) to listen to Soviet submarines. He worked with a US Navy engineer in this mission, and during their routine eavesdropping they also captured what Payne called the songs of humpback whales. The beauty of the songs impressed him, and he later collaborated with his wife, Kathryn Boynton, to identify that there was "an intentional rhyme, repetition and structure in the noises."[1]

Payne went on to record the language of whales, including fin whales, in different oceans, and he documented the language these animals shared. Whale language has dialects that are associated with different whale pods, or families. In 1970, his recordings of the whales, *Songs of the Humpback Whale,* became a global hit, and later that decade NASA included it among their Golden Record on the *Voyager* spacecraft.[2]

Payne's use of bioacoustics, which is the study of and recording of sounds from nature, including animals and humans, allowed him to create a database of whale language. This database of sounds and songs, and others like it compiled by other scholars doing fieldwork with other animals and nature, is a rich repository, very much like the Vatican archive, of information about our world. New developments in technology make novel use of this information. The introduction of generative AI onto these databases opens up the means of communication with these species. Generative AI are self-regulating and autonomous-learning AI programs. As generative AI programs move through these languages, they learn their patterns and meanings—in effect, they learn these languages, which has been impossible so far in human history, or at least for Western scientists.

Iya thought the same methods she used to help pilots connect with their planes could help babies connect with their environment. She compiles sounds from nature into a database and then identifies patterns. These patterns are reduced to codes. These codes are what form the basis for the language she's discovering. Learning the Earth language is not too different from learning one's mother tongue, she explains.

"The way language works is that a child must be exposed to it in systematic ways before six months of age, when the language is being formed," she said.

"Language is a code designed to enable people to communicate. In the first year of our life on Earth, our brain builds dedicated neural connections for this language, and we rely on it for the rest of our lifetimes. This physical network constrains our future success at acquiring a new language and constructing a new meaning. As early as in the mother's womb, we have an innate ability to perceive speech, which allows us to acquire any language we are exposed to when we are born."

The first graphemes that Iya chose to translate were of a dark bush cricket, a humpback whale, a fin whale, and what Iya called traditional songs. I wanted to know why Iya chose to feature traditional songs.

"I use songs from nations that continue to pass on songs from one generation to the next from across the globe," she said. "Traditional song preserves the intonation and accentuates sounds and words differently. Spoken language changes with time, and traditional songs, stories, and poems often remain the same throughout generations. Take traditional lullabies that would soothe anyone at any age, and no matter if they are not from the same tradition or in a familiar language."

One of the assumptions of Iya's program is that of a *panpsychism*, in which the environment, including the animals, plants, and insects that populate it, is sentient. This is also an assumption that underlies most, if not all, indigenous knowledge systems, which is probably why Iya intuitively chose to translate the music and songs of traditional societies across the globe. Iya is a scientist who utilizes scientific tools, in conjunction with her intuition, to decipher an Earth language of which Western science is not aware, but according to most indigenous cultures, the Earth and land are sentient, along with the plants and animals that populate the environment.

The "Lore" of indigenous Australians, their rituals, songs, and what Westerners consider indigenous art is a record of a language or lifeway. There are correlations with other traditional religions and folklore. An Australian scientist, upon learning of Iya's work, noticed its correlation with her country's indigenous culture.

"I wonder if some Elders [indigenous Australians] know this language and teach it, but only within their tribes. I was fortunate enough to take my son when he was very young to 'Bush School,' where we would learn many symbols and sounds and how to recognize every sentient vibrational signature, including rocks and trees. Many of the Elders in these communities use this language and interpret it for many accurate predictions, from the weather to other complex patterns."[3]

Rituals, dances, and rites, which constitute part of a lifeway language, are some ways in which traditional cultures have passed on their relationships with their land through generations. I was introduced to a North American indigenous lifeway when I was a university student. I was hired to work at a university that was reserved for indigenous Americans, called D-Q University. I helped grow and conserve indigenous plant species. I remember when a new group of young indigenous students came to live at the university. A young man about my age had a bag of corn and walked the perimeter of the grounds, which was about five acres or so. He spread the corn as he called out.

"What are you doing?" I asked.

"I'm a stranger to this land," he said. "I'm introducing myself to the spirits of the land here, so they know who I am and what my intention is. That way we can work together."

I looked through Iya's program. It fills one's senses with geometric images and sounds derived from the languages of whales, insects, and plants. I asked Iya to explain more about the significance in the images and sounds, and in the translation of sounds into image with the use of water.

"Newborn babies come here fully equipped to discern patterns and are drawn to look for them," she said.

"Babies have another unique ability. We all have it as babies and then we lose it if we don't use it or have active genes for it. It is an across-sensory modality where one sensory input is interpreted by two or more sensory modalities internally. This ability is called synesthesia. The root of the word comes from Greek, meaning to 'perceive together.' Until as recently as the beginning of this century, individuals who perceived in this way, that is, perceived sounds as colors or music as places, were thought by mainstream science to have a disorder. At best, individuals with this ability were considered to possess a vivid imagination or as very creative, if they were brave enough to express how they experienced the world. Not many shared their experiences for the fear of being judged and disadvantaged.

"Today, however, science recognizes this ability as unique, and individuals who have it have better than average executive cognitive functions. Synesthesia is proven to help in working memory, implicit learning, and allows one to resolve conflicting rules and inputs. Interestingly, native Japanese speakers have the highest prevalence of synesthesia. I don't think it is a coincidence that the Japanese culture is also considered to be innovative with respect to technology.

"For babies," she said, "the perceptual connections between a stimulus and sensation are continuously formed. For example, if the baby is stroked and the sound is produced often enough, the baby's perceptual system may code the stroke with an associated sound—hence forming one form of synesthesia. Basically, I hypothesize that the Earth language is the language that has components of synesthesia that would allow for specific connections between visual and vibrational forms. These need to be matched and learned to eventually help this new generation to pick up the Earth language."

Iya describes how the creation of neural pathways in the brains of infants would prepare them to identify or even acquire this language.

"The plan forward is to map insect and frog sounds to 2D and 3D projections that can be rotated. Babies and their parents will have systematic exposure to these images and sounds. This will aid in developing a neural network for the perception of this new language structure. It encourages forms of synesthesia and has a direct effect on executive cognitive functions and potentially, where available, the absorption of other languages in the process.

"While processing the audio files of these sounds I have noticed a pattern. The cricket sounds like a frog, the frog sounds like a bird, and the bird sounds like a whale. Even more interesting is that when I listen to the Earth's magnetic field and whilst processing the sound, I noticed, it sounds like birds! The plan is to use AI to further determine the similarities and innate codes among the calls and songs of insects, frogs, birds, and whale sounds. It is also worth exploring the NASA database of the sounds found in our solar system and space."

I listened to the sounds and watched the 3D visuals of the graphemes of the sounds. I felt like I was in an immersive art installation combined with a symphony. Cricket, whale, and bird sounds filled my ears, and their accompanying images filled my eyes.

"All patterns that I have uncovered in visual and audio form conform to the famous embedded elements of the Fibonacci sequence, which is also passed on through generations by Aboriginal traditions in Australia," Iya said.[4]

The Fibonacci sequence is a pattern of numbers that forms a symmetrical ratio that is found throughout nature, from the coils and spirals of seashells to DNA. One could perhaps think of it as the ratio of nature and beauty combined. It has never been created, but its discovery has been recorded several times in human history. Its first known written source is from the Indian mathematician Acharya Pingala, in 200 BCE. About a thousand years later, Italian mathematician Leonardo da Pisa, aka Fibonacci, scoured Pingala's work and brought recognition to the ratio in the medieval era. Tyson Yunkaporta relates how an Elder within his tribe told him about the sequence:

There is a pattern to creation. In this image you can see the way that pattern is expressed through Turtle story. A giant Turtle Spirit is hit with massive force at the center of his smooth shell. The impact makes a round section that cracks out to form another, and another. The interconnected pressure of all these round parts together forms them into hexagons, like in a sugar bag (honeybee hive). I couldn't believe it when Oldman Juma told me the sequence—one became two, then three, then five in a row along the center of the shell. Then, at the eight points where each part met, eight new parts formed. The sequence goes: 1, 2, 3, 5, 8, 13, and so on.

I laughed and said that's the Fibonacci sequence, "discovered" by an Italian mathematician around eight hundred years ago. Might add a couple of zeros to that date—it's been around longer than that. It's the pattern of creation, forming what some call the "golden ratio" that all nature is built upon, from flowers and trees to your body and even DNA.[5]

"The Earth language," Iya continued, "has a set of these patterns that are speaking with us, and we have yet to know how to decode it and teach it to others. It is right in front of our eyes, ears, and all other sensors, and we need to learn to spot the code and then figure out how to use it. Some artists and mathematicians feel this Earth language and some perceptive inventors are already learning from nature in a field called biomimetics, but we are only at the beginning in this area. We are already using this information diagnostically. The code of the lungs, for example, are fractals. In the medical field, computers are taught to tell the difference between an unhealthy and a healthy lung. The fractal dimension of the lung is different if it is healthy or if it is sick. This is one practical application of knowing and decoding this language.

"For decades, the structure of networked body elements has been considered a random pattern of flow switching between segments. By applying fractal analysis, however, it appears there is a pattern to the flow that is not random."

Iya's vision is, ultimately, to help humankind unite with each other and with our environment. She believes that people are alienated from each other and from the beings within their environment, including the universe. This vision accords with that of many people within indigenous communities around the world.

"When we speak the same language or recognize that we are from the same region on Earth," Iya said, "we instantly make a connection with one another, as if barriers are broken, if only for a moment. If the next generation learns the Earth language, we might be able to make a connection, because it is meaningful to each other in some way; it would be a great step in uniting people of Earth. It is a similar principle as when two musicians or mathematicians meet and improvise and share a common communication tool to make the instant connection."

Iya is a champion skydiver, a scuba diver, and a guide to astronauts and pilots—to those who travel to extreme environments before us and make the way safe for others who will inevitably follow. Like the great navigators of the past, she forges a seemingly impossible path that only becomes possible because she makes it. She is choosing an unknown path. I reflected, however, on her passion to teach this language to the next generation. She paves the way for future academics, and her vision is fueled by urgency. This urgency she shares with many people today. As Yunkaporta notes, "Future survival of all life on this planet will be dependent on humans being able to perceive and be custodians of the patterns of creation again, which in turn requires a completely different way of living in relation to the land."[6]

All human ancestors were once part of indigenous communities but lost a connection to land as a source of sustenance and support. Viewing land as an exploitable resource is one characteristic of nonindigenous cultures. Can technology provide one way to reverse the trend and reacquaint some people with sustainable relationships and communication with nonhuman intelligence? Iya's answer to this is "yes."

"I have been developing these ways so we can encode and decode communication and prepare our children's brains and cognition for connection and communication with other species and beings, and in the process graduate as a humanity to a better connection with Earth."

As we neared the end of our collaboration, Iya sent me a book written by two Russian scholars about their communications with dolphins. In the book was reference to a manuscript written by a French abbot of the seventeenth century, which was discovered at a monastery on the coast in southern France. I looked at a photo of the manuscript. It was an illustration of two people in the ocean with some dolphins. One had a flute. The manuscript presents instructions for how to achieve this communication. The first is intention: A person must really want to communicate and not just out of curiosity. There must be a significant reason. Second, a person must be able to be completely focused on the attempt to communicate. The manuscript states that it must be a heartfelt prayer said with sincere intention. The third instruction gave me pause. It states that a person must be able to operationalize or in some way utilize the communication, through action. It suggests that one way to do this is through sound. I looked at the flute in the image. *Ah,* I thought. The seventeenth century's technological language bridge was the flute.[7]

THE GRAY MAN

The problem is that we have no idea what to make of the bonds between humans and the spirits really present to them within the limits of our critical theories. Further theorizing along these lines is simply deflecting attention from the challenge of understanding how people meet their gods and how their gods meet them.

—ROBERT ORSI

I just wish I could stop walking through the darkness.

—GRAY MAN

ENCOUNTER

Gray Man works for a major research agency and is head of a laboratory. More than any other scientist with whom I had worked, he was most careful about what he could share, and what he could not. He edited his contributions to this book more than fifteen times.

Since the beginning of my study, I have met hundreds of

scientists and technologists who believe in UFOs. Do they know something that other people do not know about the topic? How do they reconcile their scientific pursuits with their belief in UFOs and extraterrestrials? What I learned from this community is that, contrary to the common assumption that scientists do not entertain such ideas, some of the best of them believe in extraterrestrials, nonhuman intelligences, and angels and demons—not as metaphors but as real beings. And sometimes these nonhuman entities, they believe, are not mutually exclusive categories. Gray Man related his experiences, and they reveal how these categories of beings overlap.

"I woke up to see a being hovering above me. His face was about four or five inches from my face. His eyes pierced me, I felt, and he seemed to look directly into my heart, as if he was assessing me, but it wasn't unpleasant. As I felt this kind of assessment taking place, I felt I could also see into his soul too. I felt that this being was pure, full of righteousness and incredibly powerful. His hair was long, about shoulder-length or slightly longer, and it shone pale but bright yellow to gold and looked like it was made of light. His face was so close to my face that I didn't dare move. I was completely and utterly overwhelmed, as much as a person could imagine being overwhelmed, by the idea of literally coming face-to-face with an angel or God.[1]

"This initial shock and fear were momentary. It turned into a feeling of love, peace, and joy, and the breath had been taken out of my lungs as you might experience from a huge adrenaline surge. The room, which had been dark, was lit bright with light that radiated out from his body. His body was luminous, like looking at a light bulb through a thin lampshade. His clothing was white, and he appeared to have on a sleeveless gown that could be opened at the front.

"The feeling of adrenaline soon passed, and a feeling of peace and calm came over me, and a realization that if this thing wanted me dead, I would have already been dead. I felt love and a strong connection to this being, like the love and connection you might experience with a once-in-a-lifetime best friend, the type of friend that knows you far better than even your parents. At this point I asked if I could hug this being, but he told me, "No, I have a sword, you will be injured." I did not immediately notice this sword, it was hidden; it was held vertically with the tip pushing outwardly against his clothing so that once noticing this, it became obvious that it was a sword. I wondered why he would have a sword. It was confusing to me. This being was so incredibly powerful—I did not doubt for a moment that it could easily vaporize me just by willing it.

"Time seemed to blur, and I was transported to another place, this one very dark. I felt strongly that this being was indeed sacred, holy, and pure, an angel, however it then proceeded to give me armor and weapons. This is not what I ever imagined an encounter with an angel would be like. He gave me a sword. It made no sense to me. How was this going to help me? A dark, shadowy, three-dimensional black figure appeared. It was like thick dark smoke but completely opaque. The figure was of a being that morphed and changed shape, not completely, but it did not have a fixed solid outline; it moved and flowed. I could feel it was evil. I knew the angel intended me to fight this figure, and so I did. It seemed strange to me that I was not afraid; in fact, it gave me joy to at least attempt to put an end to this dark entity not knowing whether I would perish or defeat it. For some reason, I just knew what needed to be done and so I did it. During this carnage, I was calm. This was a very unusual experience, but it felt normal, like how you might feel participating in a personal hobby. That's the feeling I got. I felt that I should be terrified, but I wasn't at all. I eventually defeated this evil being using the sword. The sword went straight through this being like swinging through air; there was no feeling of hitting something solid, but the sword seemed to disperse this dark, opaque, smoke-like matter. I sensed that the angel was pleased with me.

"I then woke up at some point soon after this. It was like waking up from being knocked out or unconsciousness, not waking from sleep. I didn't really know what to think. I felt sure this was not a dream, but what was this? I said to myself repeatedly, 'What just happened?'

"How could this be real, but it seemed so real, and what would be the purpose? I was trying so hard to make sense of it all, but I wondered why an angel would need to have a sword. Angels can be seen or not seen and are powerful. I imagined that if they were real that they could kill a demon without a sword. Was the sword for show? I didn't get it.

"Regardless of what this was, I felt overwhelming gratitude for that experience. It gave me incredible comfort at a time when I was making some big life-changing decisions. There are no words to describe the relief I felt."

Gray Man described what happened to him. He emphasized that it was not a dream. Upon looking at him, he seems the least likely person to report such an event. He's a surfer, and if you didn't know he was a scientist, you'd expect to see him on the beach with a surfboard, or with a skateboard zooming down the street. Even after two years of knowing him, I had never seen him deviate from his chosen uniform: black Vans, faded saggy jeans, and a Billabong T-shirt. His dark brown hair is buzz-cut style. He once called himself the Gray Man because he despised social media and anything that brought attention to himself. He did not allow photographs. Anything that smacked of self-promotion made him cringe.

Gray Man reminded me of another scientist surfer and UFO experiencer I'd met. In 2017 I spent four days at a small conference in California with Dr. Kary Mullis and his wife, Nancy. I had invited him to the conference because I was interested in learning about his UFO experience. Mullis had won the Nobel Prize in Chemistry for discovering the polymerase chain reaction, which was a revolutionary technology that impacted innumerable industries. He disclosed his UFO experience and his meeting with a small being that he described as an "electric raccoon" in his cabin in the mountains of Northern California. Mullis was a controversial genius who posed for photographs with his surfboard on California beaches near his house and whose views on various topics, from UFOs to climate change, did not conform to the expectations that the pubic had about scientists. Except for his disdain of being photographed, Gray Man reminded me of Dr. Mullis.

What Gray Man described to me, however, did not sound like a UFO experience.

"This being you saw sounds like Saint Michael," I said. Saint Michael the Archangel is a divine agent portrayed in the sacred scriptures of the three major Western religious traditions—Judaism, Christianity, and Islam. The angel is known to be a demon slayer and a psychopomp, which is a being that leads the souls of the dead to their afterlife destinations. He is also the guardian of children. At the time we had our conversation, Gray Man wasn't aware of this iconography, or he wasn't consciously aware of it. When I mentioned that this sounded like a dream about Saint Michael, he didn't comment, but later he told me that he wondered why I had brought it up. What would a saint have to do with an angel with a sword? He was confused about the angel he believed he saw and why it had a sword. He didn't know of the tradition of Saint Michael as an archangel and demon slayer. I had assumed that he was aware of the tradition. Yet he wasn't, and how he found out was curious.

A week after Gray Man told me about his "encounter," which is what he called it, another scientist I knew who believed in UFOs, Tyler D., sent me a few pictures of paintings that a friend of his had done of Saint Michael. I hadn't told him about Gray Man's story. The paintings were beautiful, and Tyler said that his friend, who didn't know me, told him that she thought of me and wanted me to see them. They were painted to look like frescoes, and the angel stood within a halo of blue beams with his sword in hand. The same week I noticed that a local church had placed a statue of Saint Michael in their garden. I often frequented the garden and brought my children to play and climb the trees that lined its paths. I noticed the statue but can't remember having seen it before. The statue was tall and big, taller than an average man, about six feet in height. Generally, paintings of Saint Michael represent him as being a soldier in armor with the sword, but this statue emphasized his masculinity more than any painting or prayer card I had seen. His muscles were barely contained by his armor. His face, which was calm, reminded me of how Gray Man described his angel. I was both taken aback and amused by this portrayal. Nobody but a demon would think to cross this character, I imagined.

The week began and ended with encounters of Saint Michael. At the end of the week, I was scheduled to have an interview with a pediatric therapist who partnered with my university and provided internships to our students. Her focus was on children in crisis, and she worked with my university's undergraduates as a mentor and helped them learn to support and guide children through situations that involved trauma and suffering. She was well respected for her work. As I sat across from her in her office, my eyes were drawn upward to a statue of Saint Michael prominently displayed on a shelf behind her desk. She spoke to me about her work, but I was distracted by the ominous winged presence peering down at me.

"I see you have a statue of Saint Michael," I said, after our interview was over.

The therapist looked surprised that I noticed the statue. The statue was so large that I thought it was impossible *not* to notice it.

"Yes, I do," she said. Then, with only a brief pause, she continued: "Saint Michael is a guardian and protector of children. I speak to him on a regular basis about my work. He counsels me about my young clients."

Her eyes squinted as she searched my face, probably looking for a reaction. I was surprised by her bluntness, and I hoped that I didn't show it in my expression. My work involves talking to people about their extraordinary experiences, so I'm used to hearing about them, but not during my off-hours. I considered this my off-hours even though I had been speaking to her about routine work concerning my university and training students. It had nothing to do with my research in religious studies. I was not interviewing her about her beliefs in otherworld beings.

As she spoke about her correspondence with Saint Michael, I was struck by the number of coincidences I'd experienced that week that had involved pictures or statues of him. This was the third one. I've written about synchronicity—uncanny and meaningful coincidences—and my position has been to disregard them as metaphysically meaningful. Instead, I tend to observe synchronicities as they happen and, as philosopher Friedrich Nietzsche suggests, savor the appearance of these coincidences as what they are—striking plays of chance. Nietzsche wrote of the meaningful and shocking impact of these events but cautioned his readers to avoid attributing them to God or to a divine intelligence. Instead, he recommended that we "leave the gods in peace" and admire the work of chance in our lives and laud our ability to recognize it. So far in my research into synchronicity, I've taken this position, as it seems the least laden with assumptions. Synchronicity is often the engine of spiritual and religious belief as it seems to confirm practitioner's own religious or spiritual tendencies. Even as I resist the temptation that Nietzsche suggests, I am still undecided about synchronicities. The more I study their place in people's lives, the more I'm convinced that they represent a structural component of everyone's reality, but especially of those who are naturally inquisitive about life and are open-minded.

Scholar Tyson Yunkaporta's description of what he calls "extra-cognitive" processes speaks to uncanny coincidences as part of the knowledge practices of indigenous Australian Lore. In a passage that is curiously reminiscent of Nietzsche's description of "personal providence," or synchronicities, in the philosopher's book *The Gay Science,* Yunkaporta explains this process:

> Some aspects of consciousness, knowledge, and knowledge transmission have not been explained or proven scientifically and are therefore avoided in cognitive science. I'm calling these aspects "extra-cognitive" for want of a better word. They include the messages that land and Ancestors bring to us—a bird or animal behaving strangely, a sudden wind gust, a coincidence that highlights a deep meaning or revelation, a burst of inspiration. These are the things that make knowledge processes sacred and magical.[2]

I thanked the therapist for her time and left the office.

At the end of that week of synchronicities involving Saint Michael, Gray Man called, and he was almost upset.

"Okay, something happened," he said.

"I decided to investigate what you mentioned about Saint Michael," he said. "Up until this point I had disregarded your comment. I didn't think that was going to be of any help to me, but a feeling inside of me urged me to at least learn who this Saint Michael person was. Was it an apostle? I wondered. I had no idea. I'm not one for reading, so I turned to the internet and typed in Saint Michael. I was immediately shocked by what I found. A video I clicked on described the being exactly! I got another adrenaline surge; I couldn't breathe and my heart pounded. I had to call you immediately, you were right. This is honestly freaking me out."

I could tell Gray Man was troubled and on the verge of being upset. His explanation of his physiological changes—heart beating fast—prompted me to try to calm him down. I was also confused, because I thought that he already knew about Saint Michael when I had told him. Apparently he didn't. He thought that I was trying to placate him about this experience, that I was "being nice" because I had not outright dismissed it. This information was a lot for him to handle, and he didn't know how to make sense of it.

"It's okay. People have these experiences. I agree that it is weird that you had a dream or vision of a being that looks exactly like Saint Michael," I said.

A week later he called me again. He was in the process of organizing his trip from Australia, to fly out to the United States to meet with me about the research.

"I can't believe what just happened," he said. "I went to get my passport out of the small box I had it stored in and I discovered this card at the bottom of it. Guess what it is? I will take a photo and send it to you."

He sent me the photo. It was a prayer card featuring Saint Michael. This one was probably from the late nineteenth or early twentieth centuries and shows Saint Michael dressed as a young Roman soldier. He stands on the head of Satan. In one hand he holds his sword ready to pierce Satan, and in the other hand he carries scales to weigh the souls of the dead. He looks calm. Satan is immersed in flames, and although he is defeated, he also looks calm.

"I have no idea how it got there," Gray Man said. "In fact, it took me about two hours to remember how I even came into possession of it in the first place. I got this thing twenty years ago and hadn't even looked at it once. The only reason I would have kept it was because a friend gave it to me as a gift. How it found its way into that box I have no idea. I feel speechless, in shock. This is all too incredibly weird."

These events impacted Gray Man. He interpreted the event of finding the card and many other weird things that were happening as confirmation that his experience was more than just a dream.

I wasn't exactly sure how to make sense of it, either, but I listened to him and asked a few questions for clarification. His answers made the series of events even more uncanny.

"I can believe that you didn't know who Saint Michael was, or that he is a sword-wielding demon slayer, but how then did you get this card? It's a prayer card, by the way," I said.

"My friend gave it to me. This was more than twenty years ago. He was one of my mates, but he was very troubled. He was in a maximum-security psychiatric hospital on prison grounds, actually. This is where they put severely troubled people who are too violent to keep anywhere else. He was in there. He hadn't spoken in at least two weeks. His mum called me; she was desperate. She wanted me to pray with him. I felt terrified to do this even though I knew I had to do it. Because his mum asked, I went."

"Okay," I said. "That's sad." I could feel that he was hesitant to tell me what happened. It was okay with me if he didn't, as I probably didn't want to know the story. He told me anyway.

"Yeah. It was." After a pause he continued. "My friend's mom drove us to the hospital. The hospital was on the prison grounds in Sydney. As I said, the hospital for people with serious health conditions that are too violent to be held in a regular psychiatric hospital or for prisoners with severe mental health disorders. At the entrance was security. It was kind of like going through security at the airport. I had to open my pockets and leave behind anything that could be used as a weapon. The prisoners who were there had been violent, with psychiatric conditions, not necessarily murderers, but whose behavior is disturbing, and a court determines that they need to be there. My mate did some things like run through a very thick glass door like it was nothing and did not get hurt. Stuff like that. I think that it was because of this escape from the previous hospital that he was upgraded to this new one.

"We went into a big open room. This was a room for prisoners or patients to visit with people, talk to family. There were about four guards and a few nurses. It wasn't like you see in the movies, where there is a glass or plexi-glass screen keeping you from the prisoners. We were all out there in the open.

"I sat down with him, and we started talking. At this point he had begun to talk again. We just talked about un-important things. Then his mum asked me to put my hands on his head and pray. There were probably four prison guards and a nurse and other prisoners there. I absolutely did not want to do that in front of those people. My mate asked a guard if we could have a private room . . . but no. We couldn't; we had to do it there. I was nervous, even scared, but I did it. I put my hands on his head and I prayed.

"Immediately upon putting my hands on his head I felt burning in my chest. I asked that he could be healed, that he could feel the love of God in his life, and that soon he could be out of this place and back home with his family. The prayer lasted for two minutes. After that my mate pulled away in shock. He pulled up the sleeve of his shirt and showed me goose bumps on his arms. The hair on his arms looked like they were raked with static electricity. I looked at his mum, and she had her hands on her mouth, and there were tears on her face.

"Then he smiled, stood up, and hugged me. I felt like things were already better, immediately.

"About a year later, I went around to visit him. He said he wanted to give me something. When I got to his house he pulled out this card and gave it to me. He pointed to the angel and said 'That's you.'

"I thanked him, but I was disappointed. I'm not sure what I was thinking. It's not like I wanted a gift or any-

thing, but a card with an angel on it? Although I did believe in angels, I thought the card was a misrepresentation
of what an angel might look like. I guess I decided to keep
it because it was sacred to him and he gave it to me to show
that he appreciated my friendship, the memory of what I
did with it is a complete blur. I am so shocked that it has
shown up now after twenty years."

Gray Man finished his story. I felt like how I felt when
the therapist told me about her correspondence with Saint
Michael, but this time I *was* doing research. This was a story
about an otherworld being, and it made sense that he related
it within the course of my research relationship with him,
yet it was still unexpected. This was an origin story for the
card that Gray Man found after many years, just after he
had his encounter with Saint Michael. Finding the card just
after watching videos about Saint Michael emphasized the
immediacy of his encounter with the being. The proximity
of these events unsettled him, so he reached out to me. I
was unsettled too, but not because of the string of events
that he experienced, which were interesting but could still
be explained as being latent within his unconscious. It was
conceivable that this information spilled into his waking reality for whatever reason. The finding of the prayer card
could also have been something that would happen because
of his impending travel to the United States. I was unsettled
because my own experiences seemed related to his but had
nothing to do with my unconscious or his unconscious. My
experiences were completely autonomous and therefore unexpected.

Synchronicities and uncanny events have remained on

the outskirts of Western rationalist theories for more than eighteen hundred years, starting at least with fifth-century Saint Augustine's synchronistic book encounter in a garden, which compelled him to convert to Christianity and which has been memorialized in the church hymn "Take Up and Read." Hundreds of years later, Enlightenment philosopher Immanuel Kant was so vexed by his friend Emanuel Swedenborg's alleged night journeys with angels, extraterrestrials, and precognitions that he wrote a book trying to rationally grapple with his friend's testimonies. In public Kant mocked his friend, while in private he found his friend's experiences unexplainable. Even while nineteenth-century philosopher Friedrich Nietzsche disavowed meaning or any metaphysical significance to synchronicities, his work is loaded with them. In part, this is what makes his philosophy lively and compelling to read.

Even when my inclination is to "leave the gods in peace," I am still of two minds. On the one hand I search for an underlying structure to these events, and on the other hand I'm inclined to *just get on with it* and tell the story. Perhaps telling the story will reveal pieces that will help put together the full puzzle of synchronicity. Or maybe the three coincidences that I had involving Saint Michael and that just happened to parallel Gray Man's tales of UFO encounters were just gifts by *chance* that segue into an explanation of the interpretation of UFOs as angels and demons, which is Gray Man's framework. How fitting that our guide would be none other than the ultimate demon slayer—Saint Michael the Archangel.

UFO SIGHTING: ONE

Before Gray Man became a scientist, his familiarity with his hometown's roads was limited to those that led to the ocean. He spent a good portion of his life bobbing up and down on his surfboard in the blue waves of New South Wales, Australia. When he wasn't surfing, he was riding his BMX bike, skateboarding, and watching movies related to these pursuits. The topic of UFOs never crossed his mind, so when he saw an unknown object in the sky one night as he was driving on Empire Bay Drive, he didn't interpret it to be a flying saucer.

"It was dark" he said. "I was in my car driving along Empire Bay Drive, a narrow undivided country road on the New South Wales Central Coast. Out of nowhere this giant meteor-like thing blasted through the sky above me. I don't usually curse, but on this occasion, I yelled some choice words so loud it would not surprise me if the windows in the car reverberated. The whole sky lit up like daylight; I saw the brown bark on the trees just like it was daytime. I was bracing for a sonic boom, because this thing came down so fast, like something traveling at Mach ten or faster.

"I lost sight of it behind the tree line; I estimate the trees were around forty feet tall. The object appeared to come down not more than two hundred meters away from where I was on the road. There were houses scattered throughout the forest. It was unlikely that it would burn up forty feet above the ground—no way. I was so terrified that I almost crashed my car. There was no way I was going to stop. I am *not* like those people you might see in a horror movie who stupidly walk into a forest at night to meet their predictable fate of certain death. *No way.* I was outta there as fast as possible."

Gray Man's description of the event made me laugh. Although it was scary and even emotional, he often made the events he experienced sound funny. I wasn't sure if he did this intentionally, so I didn't ask him about it. This was also a trait he had in common with Dr. Mullis, whose own description of his UFO encounter is simultaneously terrifying and hilarious.

"I felt certain that this would be reported in the national news," Gray Man said. "Nothing like that could happen without people taking notice. This was the craziest thing I'd ever witnessed in my entire life. The next week I kept a lookout for the news and there was nothing. Unbelievable."

What Gray Man did not know at the time was that there *were* reports. Self-described housewives, air traffic controllers, other young surfers, police, and many others had seen an unknown aerial object flying over the inlets known as Brisbane Waters between the years of 1994 and 1998. Gray Man had most likely been one of the witnesses to the 1994 sighting, which made national news in Australia. During a period of a few days around Christmastime people described an object that looked like a sparkling "carousel" with multiple lights that flew over their homes and yards. It stopped above various inlets and hovered over the water. Several people witnessed shafts of light appear to enter the water, suck it up, and then spit it back out into the inlet. Some people saw the water steam as if it were very hot. People watched this happen outside their backyard windows.

"All the people I spoke to had exactly the same thing to say; there was absolutely no variance whatsoever in the object that was sighted," said local police sergeant Bob Wenning. "It was a huge, round, very shiny object in the shape of a ball. At the bottom of the ball were a number of huge white lights, and this object looked like it was sucking up water. Some callers were quite frightful in their voices. You could actually hear the fear in their background, especially the fear of the people and of course animals and things that at the time were experiencing this phenomenon."[3]

The editor of *The Sun Weekly* newspaper in New South Wales published a report that said that the local police had confirmed that there was a mass sighting of an unknown object. He noted that after the story went live, hundreds of people called into the office who didn't want to be named.

"A lot of the witnesses were retired academics, some were policemen, nurses, schoolteachers, Sunday school teachers, lawyers, business people, and some of the leading business people in the area. They were all people who had everything to lose and nothing to gain by even coming forward and making a report," said Moira McGhee. Moira is a trained UFO investigator, which means she would check with air traffic control and the military to rule out weapons or aircraft exercises. After hearing the reports of hundreds of people and conducting her due diligence with respect to known aerial phenomena, she concluded that the object was an "unknown."

The reports were mostly sightings, but several of them went beyond just sightings to describe psychological effects. Sergeant Wenning describes one caller's experience.

"He told me he had been woken up from a deep sleep with thunderous noise and bright lights, dogs barking. His children came into his bedroom screaming and told him this thing was down the block of his street; you could see it, it was over the water and sucking up the water. The sound was like a million hummingbirds. He didn't know what was going on."[4]

The man was distressed. His experience included hearing a loud buzzing sound like bees or hummingbirds. There is a small subset of people who may or may not have seen a UFO but were in the vicinity where a sighting occurred and reported these effects, which include something like vivid dreams but which they insist are not dreams, much like how Gray Man described his vision of Saint Michael. They also report synchronicities. The following anonymous account of the Brisbane Waters/Gosford UFO event is typical of these reports and includes a type of synchronicity called a book encounter—in which finding a book in a coincidental way helps reframe or explain a past UFO experience.

"I was living just out of Newcastle at 21 Wallsend Road, Sandgate, across the road from the cemetery in 1994, and having mind-boggling dreamlike experiences that were not dreams. I was still somewhat ambiguous especially confiding in others when they give you that look as they quickly depart your company or gaslight you. One day I was walking up Hunter Street in the Newcastle Mall and was intuitively compelled and drawn into a bookshop, and behold; depicted in *The Gosford Files* was the exact location and date of a UFO that was observed hovering over the house I was living in, confirming I was not just dreaming."

Former US Navy intelligence officer Matthew Roberts experienced similar effects in 2015 while he was on board the aircraft carrier the USS *Theodore Roosevelt*. During his time on the ship, navy pilots captured a video of an unknown aerial phenomenon that resembled small Tic Tac candies. The objects flew in and around the pilots' planes and exhibited flight patterns that these military personnel believed to be impossible for known aerial technology, like turning 180 degrees in midflight. The video was later released to *The New York Times* in a now-famous series of news disclosures of the US military's "black" or secret programs alleged to have been created to study UFOs. In correspondence with Roberts, I asked him his thoughts on why only a small set of the people on board both the *Roosevelt* and the other carrier whose personnel shared these experiences, the USS *Nimitz*, reported psychological effects.

"The really important connection there was that the initial experience spoke to me on a level that it did not speak to others," he said.

"In terms of how this all works, I was deeply affected by it. I had done all the right psychological work necessary for this change to begin within me, and that's why it impacted me as it did. Because I had done the psychological work, there was some level of subconscious communication between the phenomenon and myself. You could imagine it being like running a magnet over different metals and seeing which ones move. I believe they were in those craft and sending out a psychic message to see who would receive it. Since I had done all the appropriate psychological work, the signal was loud and clear to me, but others who hadn't done that work were completely blocked off by it."[5]

Roberts came to view this event as an initiation into a radically spiritual way of life that he could only understand through reading books about Greek mythology and religion. He read the works of Plato, books by pioneering psychologist Carl Jung, the popular work of Joseph Campbell, and the information in the work of technology/venture capitalist and UFO researcher Jacques Vallée. With respect to the latter, he told me that Vallée's work was helpful, and he wanted to relay his thanks to Jacques.

"Hearing the call caused me to dig into the topic. I dug in where I knew I would find answers. This set up the knowledge I needed to navigate the rest of the initiation. Previous to that I had what I thought were just strange dreams. Vallée really opened my eyes to the experiences, where I was unsure of time (some were that way but others were very much linear), but also the heavy religious undertones and symbolism of the experience. It was in reading Vallée that I came to understand that they weren't strange vivid dreams. So next time you speak to him, you'll have to thank him for me. Mission accomplished for him! I was an atheist, so I really pushed back on those undertones because I found them difficult to accept until the evidence became undeniable."

Dreams that aren't really dreams. Atheists who become religious, or at the very least, intensely spiritual. References to myths that seem like they're real and to beings that were once considered metaphoric but seem strangely literal. I had heard this all before. These are the elements of religious experiences. I *used* to think these experiences were religious conversions. Today I look at them differently. I now understand these experiences as common to the awakening of a human being to the cosmos in which they live, like fish that swim around in a fishbowl and suddenly wake up to the reality of water.

Gray Man's experiences did not just feature angels, but also things that he identified as evil, including aliens. In this way, he was like many of the experiencers I've met. Generally, if a person experiences a sighting of a UFO or orb, they often have other nonordinary experiences. The UFO event is like a door that opens a person to a nonordinary world.

4

GRAY MAN II

Some people have experiences that are so strange, they attribute them to alien intervention of some kind. Close encounters of the first kind, second kind, third kind, etc., as though alien intervention would always fall into certain categories. I had one of those experiences myself. To say it was aliens is to assume a lot. But to say it was weird is to understate it. It was extraordinarily weird.

—KARY MULLIS

EVENT TWO

In the early 2000s, Gray Man worked as a scientist and attended a Christian church. He met a retired man who became a friend. The man, who was in the same field as Gray Man, loved to talk to him about a lot of different things, mostly related to work. Gray Man was good at listening, and if he could avoid speaking, he did. This is how he found out some interesting information from his new friend.

On one occasion the man and his wife invited Gray Man

over to his house for dinner, and Gray Man readily accepted. It was there that the retired man revealed that his work had been so secret that when he traveled to meetings by plane, his briefcase was handcuffed to his wrist. Gray Man also found out that his friend and he shared a similar specialty with regard to their shared work—they both worked on the scientific aspects of aeronautics. The man's affiliations were with well-known aeronautics companies.

The man's wife was a gracious host, and they had invited three people as guests from church—Gray Man and two other people, including a young woman.

"We were having a pleasant discussion, and then, out of nowhere, this young woman said, 'What about UFOs!' This felt incredibly awkward, and I felt embarrassed for her partly because of the topic but also in the way she interrupted my friend and the polite conversation we were having. I kept staring at my plate of food and hoped my friend could manage this situation without further embarrassment.

"This man," Gray man said, "who probably had the highest clearance you could have, replied, 'Yes, they are real.'

"To say I was surprised is probably an understatement. I looked at his wife for any sign or indication that her husband's story was a joke, but there was none. The wife just sat there as if her husband was talking about the weather outside. She showed no sign of embarrassment or awkwardness with her husband's remarks."

At that small dinner party Gray Man's interpretation of events in his life changed. He began to reassess some of things that happened to him. He started to look into the topic of UFOs, and he noticed that people, for the most part, ignored the paranormal and supernatural aspects that also occur when people see UFOs. He felt that these aspects were not just part of the experience of sighting a UFO but were key to understanding the nature of the phenomena.

"If these events were just the case of an extraterrestrial contact experience, then why would all these other weird paranormal effects occur along with it? When people landed on the Moon, I am reasonably certain they didn't use a Ouija board to communicate with ground control on planet Earth. Why didn't someone save the inventor of the radio some time and headache by letting him know 'there is no need to reinvent the wheel; we have a Ouija board.'

"Upon returning to Earth these astronauts became the equivalent of an alien race visiting planet Earth. Did their families or colleagues start experiencing paranormal activity in their homes after meeting with the astronauts? Somehow, I think not. Then why is it that virtually all of the UFO/alien contact experiences that I am aware of contain some type of paranormal phenomena that goes along with it?"

Gray Man was adamant that these experiences were not extraterrestrial but somehow linked to spirituality or religion.

"If you actually look at the reports of UFOs, you see that a lot of weird stuff happens, dark stuff, stuff that is not cool. Even in the movie *Close Encounters of the Third Kind,* which is supposed to be about an extraterrestrial visitation, weird things happen. In one scene a vacuum cleaner runs amok and begins to vacuum stuff up on its own. It vacuums the house by itself. This is well before vacuum cleaners could do this. Dolls and other toys operate on their own. The main premise of the story is that a guy who was in the vicinity of the UFO gets targeted and starts to make sculptures of the location of Devil's Tower. What a weird pun on words, by the way, and it should not go unnoticed. I mean, this is all so dark. Why isn't anybody talking about this? Instead, the movie is seen as a story about extraterrestrials. It actually does a great job of revealing a lot of scary dark parts of the UFO events, but many people don't talk about those."

One of the things that Gray Man felt that his UFO research put into perspective were dreams he had had throughout his life. He described frequent bouts of sleep paralysis, lucid dreams, and other types of dreams for which he had no explanation. Sleep paralysis is a physiological condition that happens to some people when they sleep. People suffering from this condition report being aware that they are asleep, or being wakened from sleep but unable to move. They also report having what some sleep researchers report as hallucinations and a feeling of suffocation. It is a very scary temporary condition that affects up to 50 percent of people from all cultures, and it has been described throughout history. Dr. David Hufford, a folklorist and medical doctor, spent many years traveling throughout the world collecting stories of sleep paralysis. He noted that it is often accompanied by the feeling or knowledge that a being, perhaps a child, or in some cultures, a "hag," is walking toward the person who is asleep. The sleeping person feels threatened and tries to wake up but cannot because they're paralyzed. Researchers, such as Ryan Hurd, have identified ways of waking oneself from these terrifying sleep states, such as clenching one's fist.

Sometimes, however, dreamers experience something other than sleep paralysis. Gray Man describes such an episode.

"I was in bed and I woke up, as conscious as I am now," Gray Man said.

"There was a hooded man standing by my bed, and he wore a white mask. I felt with absolute certainty that if I didn't do something pretty quick, I was going to be dead—murdered. He was going to kill me. Well, I assumed he was going to kill me. I kept repeating to myself in my head, 'Calm down, calm down, calm down.' I was so angry, I was prepared to kill this guy. I was doing my absolute best to slow my heart rate down and develop enough rage and anger in my mind to do what needed to be done—absolutely destroy this person. I jumped off my bed and lunged for the guy. He completely dissolved, disappeared. I was so terrified that I ran out of my room and turned on all the lights in the house. I am not sure what to think about it; it certainly was not a dream. I was wide awake, completely alert, and terrified. I paused and thought about what needed to be done and then acted, the same way you would act if someone broke into your home at night."

Gray-colored aliens visited his night visions. He described another occasion of a lucid dream event.

"On this occasion, I cannot say with absolute certainty that I was awake, because the experience ended with me waking up, but it did not feel like a dream. It was like I had woken up and then had been knocked out unconscious and then woke up a second time after regaining consciousness. Anyway, this is what happened: There were about three small gray beings. They looked like the gray aliens that people talk about. They were about three feet tall, with big black eyes and big heads, and they may each have had a mouth. The feeling I got from them was that they were purely evil, filled with pure evil. I tried to use my mind to fight them off. I commanded them in my mind in the name of Jesus to be gone.

"These were not dreams. I'm certain that they were not dreams or nightmares because I've had those before, and they never caused me to coach myself on what to do when the gray aliens came back. This certainly didn't feel like a dream. A nightmare or dream is soon forgotten, but you don't forget these experiences; they create intense fear to the point of coaching yourself on what to do if the beings come back. I didn't even care if I had no chance of surviving a fight with them, I just didn't want to give them the pleasure of having complete control over me. I would rather die fighting than allow that to happen again. When nighttime approached, I would be on edge. I would prepare my mind that no matter how frightened I might become, I would take care of the situation. I didn't want to feel unprepared if I had another encounter with them; I was going to have vengeance if it happened. It wasn't like I was certain they would be back, it was more about the fact that this kind of experience is so frightening that if you haven't properly prepared your mind in advance, you will have absolutely no chance. The fear is unbelievable. I did everything I could to feel like I was ready. I did this every night for maybe four weeks or so.

"Eventually, the feeling of dread and fear of seeing them gradually left. I haven't had a repeat experience of that in many years."

Gray Man's nighttime terrors reminded me of several discussions I had with Kary Mullis about his own encounters with a small being near his cabin in the California coastal forest. They are similar in that Gray Man and Kary encountered a similar type of being, and their reactions to this were also similar. Kary wrote about his account, and he and I spoke about it on several occasions. Kary is among the smartest and funniest people I've met. He abhorred what he called sloppy thinking, and I saw him unintentionally intimidate people with his extroverted brilliance. He challenged me about my interest in UFOs, and I challenged him back by reciting his own story about his encounter. He liked that. Because I wasn't trying to offer hard conclusions about the topic but collect as much information about it as possible, he thought that the work was valuable and wanted to attend more of the small conferences I had organized. During our talks he opened up about his encounter. One night, on his way to the outdoor bathroom near his cabin in the mountains of Northern California, he encountered what he later described as an electric raccoon:

The path down to the john heads west and then takes a sharp turn to the north after a few earthen steps. Then it runs level for about twenty feet. I walked down the steps, turned right, and then at the far end of the path, under a fir tree, there was something glowing. I pointed my flashlight at it anyhow. It only made it whiter where the beam landed. It seemed to be a raccoon. I wasn't frightened. Later, I wondered if it could have been a hologram, projected from God knows where.

The raccoon spoke. "Good evening, doctor," it said. I said something back, I don't remember what, probably, "Hello." The next thing I remember, it was early in the morning. I was walking along a road uphill from my house. What went through my head as I walked down toward my house was, "What the hell am I doing here?" I had no memory of the night before. I thought maybe I had passed out and spent the night outside. But nights are damp in the summer in Mendocino, and my clothes were dry, and they weren't dirty.[1]

When I asked him to speak more about the raccoon, Kary told me that it looked like it had been plugged into an electric socket, as it was radiating light. After this encounter he lost memory of the event until the next morning, when he "woke up." His sentiment about the event was the same as Gray Man's on many levels. He knew that he wasn't dreaming. He knew what he encountered was real and that it had some control over him. He was afraid of his own property, which he had previously loved. He was angry and wanted to fight back at all costs at whatever had greeted and seemingly abducted him. Later that week he took a gun into the forest and littered the trees and bushes with bullets where he had had his encounter.

Dr. Kary Mullis passed away in 2019. I would love to have introduced him to Gray Man, as I knew they would enjoy talking about all types of things and especially surfing. I asked Gray Man to elaborate on the connections he drew between his framework of the supernatural and the framework of UFOs. He wanted to make sure that I understood that he thought that the UFO-related events that happened to him were about evil, and most importantly, fighting evil. This was especially important to him as a father. His desire to protect his children from these events was overwhelming. When he related how he felt in the face of events that happened to his children, he paused several times. Was he regaining his composure? I couldn't tell. It made me sad to listen and watch.

"I have two young children with special needs, one is nonverbal autistic. Having severely autistic children is fraught with many dangers; they are not safe on their own for even one minute. Because of this my son needed to sleep with me in my bedroom. Anyway, on one occasion when we woke up, I went to the bathroom and while I was brushing my teeth I noticed that my shirt was on inside out and back to front, and I thought I was such an idiot to have done that, but it wasn't until later when I took off my son's warm coat that I noticed underneath that his top was also on back to front, except his top was a buttoned top and all the buttons were still done up. At that point I knew something strange was happening in my home. There is no way he could have done that; he was five or six at the time and severely autistic. Even today at the age of twelve he is incapable of dressing himself.

"In addition to these events, other strange things happened in the home that could be described as poltergeist activity. On one occasion a door opened and closed several times throughout the day and night, and other bizarre events occurred. After a while it just stopped.

"It's like this phenomena takes pleasure in mocking you. It's like something is saying to us, 'We can do anything we want with you, and you can't do anything about it.'

"In my opinion the data does not point to ET. This does not appear to be just a situation of space travelers from another planet visiting Earth. If this was the case, why should we expect to observe paranormal effects accompanying these sightings?"

Through his research, Gray Man learned about the history of the American space program and the work of Jack Parsons. Parsons is the rocket scientist who is often credited with being the father of modern-day rocketry. He was associated with a colorful and motley group of people who lived in California in the early twentieth century. Among the members of the group were Satanist Aleister Crowley and the founder of Scientology, L. Ron Hubbard. To say this combination of individuals created a lot of drama is an understatement. Parsons utilized ritual magic to allegedly contact beings from other dimensions, or extraterrestrials. He used sex magic, engaged in orgies, and performed rituals inspired by an eclectic religion allegedly channeled by Crowley, called Thelema. Parsons owned a compound on the outskirts of Los Angeles and he kept his neighbors unhappy and the local police busy with his parties, revelry, and his pursuits in the creation of rocket technologies—which was funded by the United States to develop.

Gray Man explained that he felt that Parson's magic may have actually worked.

"I personally think that in all likelihood Parson's magic may have actually worked. If it didn't work, why would a scientist or engineer engage in such activities and risk losing his credibility and position at work. I am surprised that he was never forced to undergo a psych evaluation and booted out of there. This was the guy on the cutting edge of science and engineering at the time, and he was performing bizarre rituals to try and contact beings from who knows where. All of the people he associated with were pretty 'out there,' even Wernher von Braun, who is a decorated scientist thought to be the father of the United States space program. Von Braun, though, gave credit to Parsons as the person who was the real genius behind off-planet travel. During World War II the Germans created a concentration camp to develop von Braun's ideas, his calculations mainly, into weapons. Late in his life, von Braun became a Christian. Why do you think he did that?"

Gray Man referenced Mittelwerk, a concentration camp-manned factory created for the sole task of turning von Braun's technologies into weapons. Von Braun worked for the National Socialist German Workers' Party, or the Nazis, during World War II. After the war he was moved to the United States to work for the US space program through a secret operation now known as Project Paperclip.[2] The Nazis used free labor to build their rocket program. They worked the inmates literally to death, and they died in wretchedness. The weapons built at Mittelwerk focused on weaponized rockets like the V-2. Historian Tracy Dungan points out, "More people died building the V-2 rockets than were killed by it as a weapon."[3]

"Honestly," Gray Man continued, "why would these people engage in these ritual activities if those activities didn't work? They were doing stuff that other people don't do and in fact wouldn't dare do. They engaged in these activities because they most likely worked for them. What's the alternative? That somehow they were irrational, delusional people, while at the same time being some of the best problem solvers on the planet, requiring a high degree of critical thinking, an excellent understanding of math, and a very good working knowledge of other various fields of science to solve the problems they were working on?

"They were smart people. I find it incredibly difficult to believe these people could engage in such ridiculous practices while working on some of the most secret and advanced research projects at the time. It seems ridiculous that they would participate in such activity if it didn't work for them. If it did work, then it wasn't coming from ET, and it wasn't coming from God. It was coming from something that is not God and not ET. I assume von Braun knew what he participated in was incredibly dangerous and worried him so much that he converted to Christianity late in life."

Within the field of the study of UFOs, there is a subset of researchers who believe that UFOs are a demonic force. Some researchers, such as author Nick Redfern, even suggest that there are some people in government programs who believe UFOs are demons and that they are actively engaged in thwarting UFO research because of this belief. Some members of the Invisible College—the group of scientists who began to study UFOs in secret with Allen Hynek throughout the 1960s until the present—are also very religious. I have met most of the members of the Invisible College and have worked with some of them. I was surprised to learn that some of them practice Catholic and Episcopal devotions, which are not just run-of-the-mill prayers that one engages in every Sunday at church, but are intentional and specific spiritual rituals meant to cleanse and align one's soul with God.

Gray Man is not unique in understanding his UFO experiences within the framework of religion, and he is not unique in how these experiences determine his life and lifestyle. Like the members of the Invisible College who practice devotions, Gray Man prays and commits himself to a strict religious practice. He also exhibits a characteristic that Matthew Roberts discusses regarding his own experiences. Roberts described not caring whether he lived or died, and he thought that this somehow prepared him for his initiation through his experience on board the USS *Roosevelt*. On many occasions Gray Man expressed a similar sentiment. With respect to experiencing the phenomena, he remarked that if it killed him, he'd be okay with that, as long as he died fighting.

"Sometimes I think I would die or be killed. This never affected me. *Do me the favor*—that's what I thought."

For many experiencers, the UFO phenomenon is a way of life that they never chose but nonetheless endure. Part of the horror for Gray Man and other people like him is that the boundaries between day and night, dreams and waking life are so permeable that they sometimes seem indistinguishable. After years of listening to their encounters, I couldn't help but reflect on the famous director of horror films Wes Craven and the comments he made about the inspiration for his most well-known franchises. Sadly, it tells the story of a young boy whose parents didn't believe his night terrors were real. The consequences were tragic:

> I'd read an article in the *L.A. Times* about a . . . young son [who] was having very disturbing nightmares. He told his parents he was afraid that if he slept, the thing chasing him would get him, so he tried to stay awake for days at a time. When he finally fell asleep . . . they heard screams in the middle of the night. By the time they got to him, he was dead. He died in the middle of a nightmare. Here was a youngster having a vision of a horror that everyone older was denying. That became the central line of *Nightmare on Elm Street*.[4]

UFOS AND RELIGION FROM THE PERSPECTIVE OF INFORMATION TECHNOLOGIES

After the Pentagon report on UFOs was released in June 2021, academic researchers formed groups to study the phenomena. Most of the new researchers approached the topic as if the study of UFOs had just begun. They weren't aware of the long history of ufology and the study of UFOs by scientists who worked quietly or by those who worked for the government in secret programs. Instead, they focused on hard science and assumed they were dealing with crafts that worked within the frameworks of traditional physics. The supernatural and paranormal aspects of the phenomena were and are still largely ignored.

Jacques Vallée was one of the original proponents of the theory that the phenomena should be studied from a framework that included a religious *and* technological lens. As such, his work defied normal categories of the study of UFOs in that he pushed the limits of what had and has been thought—and this was in the 1960s.

"When the underlying archetypes are extracted," he wrote, "the saucer myth is seen to coincide to a remarkable degree with the fairy-faith of Celtic countries [. . . religious miracles . . .] and the widespread belief among all peoples concerning entities whose physical and psychological descriptions place them in the same category as the present-day ufonauts."[5]

Research into the UFO phenomena benefits from a religiously informed interpretive framework. As Gray Man's example reveals, many people who see UFOs experience supernatural or unwanted paranormal events, such as time distortion, sleep paralysis, and a feeling that the entities they see are evil or divine. They experience meaningful coincidences that appear to be intended just for them—synchronicities. Like some Catholic saints of bygone eras, experiencers sometimes levitate and report being floated upward or around their rooms.

In his comparison of modern-day UFO events with religious traditions, Vallée presaged important theoretical and societal developments. First, he used the burgeoning models of information technology as an interpretive framework to study religious events and the impact that supernatural characters—deities, angels, and demons, and in the modern era, UFOs—have on populations. This allowed him to identify how the phenomena work on a metamythological level. By doing so, he postulated the existence of something that appears to act as a metaintelligence that regulates human behavior on an individual (micro) and cultural (macro) level.

Religion and technology are not generally discussed together because they have been thought to be of two completely different categories and worlds. The significance of Vallée's interpretive move is that it complicates the assumed objective reality of religious characters. Scholars of the Enlightenment and the post-Enlightenment demanded material proof for religious belief; they wanted to put an angel under a microscope. But deities and supernatural characters do not exist in the ways in which we assumed they existed.

Currently, "hard science" cannot explain how, or even where, matter exists. The question of the reality of religious deities persisted in the twentieth century because scholars wanted objective proof of them. The type of proof that was required assumed that they must be substantial—meaning material. However, developments in science and technology have made the question of proof that corresponds to substance less easy to maintain. Vallée observed the UFO phenomena's effects on culture, people, and he observed objective evidence, such as blips on radar that correlated with reported sightings. These observations led him to identify a pattern of input and response, and he described the phenomena as a control system. He used information technology and elements of behavioral psychology to identify a schedule of reinforcement. He forecasted that future tools of information technology would offer more insights into the intelligence he ascribed to religion and to modern UFOs:

> UFOs and related phenomena are "the means through which man's concepts are being rearranged." Their ultimate source may be unknowable, at least at this stage of human development; what we do know, according to Vallée, is that they are presenting us with continually recurring "absurd" messages and appearances which defy rational analysis but which nonetheless address human beings on the level of myth and imagination.
>
> "When I speak of a control system for planet earth," he says, "I do not want my words to be misunderstood: I do not mean that some higher order of beings has locked us inside the constraints of a spacebound jail, closely monitored by psychic entities we might call angels or demons. I do not propose to redefine God. What I do mean is that mythology rules at a level of our social reality over which normal political and intellectual action has no power."[6]

The question scholars asked in the twentieth century about how and why religions persist or how deities could possibly be real to believers has given way to questions about how information exists, as it appears that deities, at the very least, exist as information. New tools allow people to assess billions of data that reveal how populations react or respond to input; they can even predict these responses. With such a macro view of behavior, one can identify how modern vehicles for the transmission of mythologies—entertainment, social media, movies, and video games, where contemporary gods meet, fight, and interact with viewers and players, for example—influence behavior on a mass scale.

* * *

Gray Man flew to the United States. Through experiencers like him, I became much more educated about the paranormal and supernatural aspects of the UFO phenomena. Sadly, because of Gray Man's presence in the United States, I also lost an affiliation with a colleague who had made a significant impact on my understanding of the UFO phenomena.

Tyler D. had been an inspiring influence on my understanding of UFOs and their physical characteristics. I had worked with him and our colleague Dr. Garry Nolan on several projects, one of which involved going to an alleged UFO crash site in New Mexico. I had worked with him for six years. We traveled to the Vatican and the Vatican Observatory to conduct my research, and it was natural for me to discuss everything related to the phenomena with him to get his perspective and input. When I told him about a materials scientist from Australia, his usual casual and happy demeanor shifted. To put this in context, Tyler was required by his employer to report activities with international people. He explained that as long as Gray Man lived in Australia, he would continue to work with me. If Gray Man came to the United States and if I continued to work with him, my working relationship with Tyler would be over.

At the time, I didn't understand. I wanted to know why we all couldn't work together.

There were only a few times I have seen Tyler angry. This was one of those times. He didn't raise his voice; that wasn't his style. He paused for an interval that was long enough to make his point. He turned his face and said with very little emotion and an underlying tone of disdain, because I hadn't yet understood, "The point is not to figure it out. We are not meant to figure it out."

I thought that "figuring it out" was the point of the research. To put this in context, this exchange happened in another era, a few years prior to 2021 and before the Pentagon released its report of its UFO activities. Perhaps, in this new era, post-2021, researchers from around the world can work together to figure it out. We shall see.

5

THE SOLDIER

Terrestrial thought is becoming conscious that it constitutes an organic whole, endowed with the power of growth, and both capable of, and responsible for, the future.

—Pierre Teilhard de Chardin

On Día de los Muertos, the Day of the Dead, otherwise known as All Saints Day, Catholics all over the world give thanks and respect to those who have died and were martyred for their hope and action for a just world. They also ask for intervention from the deceased to help in their efforts to continue the creation of a just world. These martyrs are known as saints because they have transitioned into the world beyond the physical world. On this day it is believed that the separation between the living and the dead is open and that communication between them flows freely. On this day I noticed my former student's post on social media, indicating that he was about to travel to England, and it would be the first time since he had been a soldier—many years ago, but not that many—that he would be traveling outside of the United States. Jose mentioned that his body did not know the difference between then and now, which meant that his body thought he was going to war to fight a battle.

On this day Jose posted and publicly asked for the intervention and support of Pierre Teilhard de Chardin, a French Jesuit priest, who is not a saint by official Catholic recognition but is a saint to many, including me. He was a soldier in World War I and was awarded the highest French order of merit one can attain as a soldier and as a civilian. His experience of direct combat on the front woke him up to an organic network that he later termed the "noösphere." In the midst of trench warfare, he witnessed a battle of boys who died and left their surviving brothers devastated and spattered in blood and tears, and here he saw "Earth's soul" rise.

Chardin described Earth's soul, or the noösphere, as the culmination of a process of human evolution that proceeds from the geosphere and eventually encompasses a biosphere of human thought, sentiment, and information. It is "a network or a world network of economic and psychic affiliations that is being woven at an ever-increasing speed which envelops and constantly penetrates more deeply within each of us." It is an organic development and some have seen in Chardin's vision the internet. Yet Chardin did not separate humans from their environment, instead he wrote that they create it and are re-created by it. The noösphere is "life setting out upon a second adventure from the springboard it established when it created humankind."[1] It is the next stage of the evolution of human intelligence. It could be the next branch of *Homo sapiens*.

A day passed and I called Jose. He had not left the country yet.

"I saw your post about Chardin. I like that you called upon him on Día de los Muertos," I said.

I wanted to acknowledge that I understood Jose's reasoning, as I thought it was inspired. Strangely, it turned out that while he did ask for Chardin's intervention, he forgot it was Día de los Muertos, so his post on that day was a coincidence.

"Ahh. I forgot it was that day," he said.

There was silence as we both took that in. It was as significant to him as it was to me. Of all the days in which Jose had lived, he chose that one day to ask for saintly intervention, and not just from anyone, but from a Jesuit soldier and philosopher who predicted a coming choice for humanity—to live with or die by technology.

I've known Jose for ten years. He is a young man, and when I met him as an undergraduate student in my university department, he was a marine who had just returned from Afghanistan. I recall seeing him sitting in the very back corner of a large class I taught, as if he didn't want to be seen. He was, actually, hard to miss. Among the sea of bright colors worn by my students from the South, he stood out in plain black and white clothes, wearing black Buddy Holly–style glasses. There was something familiar about him, but I wasn't sure what it was. I ascribed the feeling to having a common home state, California. Jose had spent some of his youth in Los Angeles, and his style reflected that. But I learned that I was wrong about his hometown.

I found out that he grew up in New Mexico, in a *pueblito* called Artesia, about forty-five minutes from Roswell.

"That's the confirmation I needed, Diana," he said, referring to the coincidence. "I've been asking for a sign all week, a sign that I am on the right path."

I was still taking in the layers of meanings associated with the connection, the day, and the request for help. If there was one person I knew who understood Chardin's philosophy from the inside out—who lived it daily—it was Jose.

"Jose, wow, you didn't *know*? That's weird," I said. "He's your saint—a philosopher and a soldier. He foresaw a tech takeover and a fork in the road for humanity, way before the computer or the internet."

"Yeah. I know."

Jose was on his way to be interviewed for a docuseries on which I had been a consultant. It was about UFOs. Jose, though, made it very clear that he couldn't stand the topic. He made this known to me and to the production team members who were filming the docuseries. Apparently, that didn't dissuade them in the least from wanting to interview him, as Jose's life had been punctuated by UFO events. Before looking into those, however, it is necessary to provide the context of a life of UFO contact. Jose, like many experiencers, does not just experience consistent UFO events, he also sees them as natural occurrences that dot the landscape of a life imbued with spiritual meaning and choices. They are not events to be separated and extracted from his life and then studied. Many experiencers see the UFO event as natural and they view the public hysteria around it as unnecessary and even harmful. It is a distraction from their mission, and almost all experiencers have a mission.

If Matthew Roberts, who called his own UFO event an initiation, were to see a timeline of Jose's life, he might say that Jose's initiation started when he was just a child, before he had a choice of whether he wanted to be initiated. Now Jose's on the far side of initiation, and there is nothing he can do about it except to reach for the future.

To reach for the future is not an easy path. When a person chooses to do that, it means that the person's *present* is not, nor has been, optimal. Reaching for the future is a choice between two options—usually between whether to live or to die. This characterization is not an exaggeration. The mental health of United States military veterans, and of American youth in the early twenty-first century, is at a point of crisis. Suicide is the fourth leading cause of death among teenagers, and among young veterans it is the second leading cause of death. Among the students who filter through my department, I've observed that while all of them are very smart, most travel through to pick up a degree that will help them gain entrance to graduate or law school. Some, like Jose, come because they recognize that the red pill of philosophy and religious studies is option one in the two options they have. It was certainly that for Jose.

Within the first year of being a university student, Jose organized a weekly meeting of military veterans from across the university. They met in the department's philosophy seminar room and shared their stories. The intention of the weekly meetings was to help the veterans avoid suicide. Jose became a conduit of meaning, and thus hope, for

a growing group of young men and women. He also organized a project to help at-risk children. He found a plot of
land and, through a series of negotiations, he was able to
start a sustainable agricultural project that helped the children in two ways. First, it allowed them to stay off-line and
to grow their own food. Second, it allowed them to learn
business skills. They grew chili peppers and sold the sauce
to sustain the farm.

What most people don't understand about philosophy is
that it is not "just" information. Rather, it is power and a
force. Learning philosophical traditions produces powerful
effects in the lives of those who receive it. I learned that
many philosophers acknowledged that, for them, philosophy was not a choice but a necessity, and some even said
that it was the necessary choice that prevented their suicide.
I was never surprised to find this out, yet I was surprised
to learn how many philosophers stated it publicly. Hannah
Arendt, a philosopher from Germany who was interned in
and then escaped from a women's concentration camp in the
1940s because she was Jewish, wrote a poem when she was
seventeen, years before her internment, that illustrates the
sentiment of how one reaches for the future:

> *The hours run down*
> *The days pass on.*
> *One achievement remains:*
> *Merely being alive.*

Philosophy, for some, is literally *life*.

*   *   *

I've observed that those who endeavor to reach for the future are sometimes richly rewarded. One year after Arendt wrote that poem, she met the philosopher Martin Heidegger. Through him, and importantly not *because of* him, she received the tradition of thinking, or dialectical philosophy, which involves being actively engaged in thinking and reflection to the point where it becomes a moral sense. Like Jose, she had done the necessary work of reaching for the future, so she received and greatly improved upon the tradition of thinking she received from Heidegger. Her legacy lives through her books, interviews, and the people who knew her. As her friend, philosopher Karl Jaspers, noted, "Philosophizing *is real* as it pervades an individual life at a given moment."[2] I was privileged to see philosophy enter and pervade Jose's life. I also benefited from it, as he transitioned from a soldier to a philosopher-soldier, and to someone whose opinion I came to trust.

What I have termed "reaching for the future" is a way of life. Jose learned it through his military training. Like Chardin, he was on the frontline of a war in which he witnessed the deaths of people who were his brothers in every way except by blood. He was part of a small squadron of men who, by necessity and through the specter of the ever-present threat of death by sniper or explosion, were highly attuned to each other and their environment. Jose felt the electric current that Chardin called "Earth's soul." Before ever hearing about Chardin's philosophy, Jose identified this current as a network that linked him to the mental, physical, and emotional states of his brothers, and to information about the Afghanistan terrain and people. The information it provided was life-giving. He knew who to trust, where to go, and which areas to leave. He avoided explosions and snipers. His brothers called him "lucky." He told me that the network is what kept him alive. It didn't keep all his brothers alive, sadly. This fact is Jose's scar and he bears it today. It is also his connection to the network and the motivation to live.

Years after Jose graduated from my university, I vented my frustration about the state of the world, and how even though I felt hopeless, I was "functionally" hopeful because my actions were predicated on a belief that they would help people and not hurt people. The conversation that ensued from this complaint outlined Jose's assessment of the current state of our nation and the meta-warscape, which is virtual and physical. According to Jose, we are targets *and* soldiers in a war of which most people are unaware. He did empathize with my feeling of hopelessness, but he reminded me that people have been here before, and through them we learn, we correct, and we continue.

"In medieval Japan, the *living dead* was a way of life for Samurai soldiers," Jose said. "It is a rare thing to see that today. It is also disastrous without a guide and team. For example, during World War II the atrocities committed by Japanese soldiers were unfathomable. It was Bushido, the ethical code of the Samurai soldiers, that enabled them to commit those atrocities. The ever-present reality of their death pushed them to a mental state that you describe. My point is that God has to be central in this pathway, or one could get lost. I think most people today understand this but have no real leader. I also think this mode of thinking is only understood by warriors who have discipline.

"I know you are aware of the complexity and players who run this world," he said.

"When you bring it up, there's sadness in your tone. I read it like this: you think, *This is an unattainable goal.* . . . *I can do nothing but try.* That is right, you can only try. But you seem to think that that is something trivial, to just *try.* When in reality, that is it, that is the answer. When a person tries beyond knowing if what they try will work, they commit *in absolute* to a cause, which requires them to be a leader subject to the burden of command. This is a lonely road because you cannot entirely express fears, worries, despair, happiness, or joy. This is why I hate being in leadership positions. To be a cornerstone of hope requires great individual sacrifice across all situations and experiences, and depending on what you are fighting for, death lingers. But it has to come from you with complete knowledge of all the good and bad that comes with it; as my old man used to tell me, 'You can't be a weekend warrior in a war.'"

I have no idea if Jose's past created the person that he is presently, or if he was born a philosopher-soldier; perhaps it is a combination of both. I do know that Jose was born into a war that is being waged here, in the United States, and he has never left it. His teaching, which I finally understood after ten years of resistance, is that "in the battlefield, we have defeated racism." Jose told me that the battlefield is a space of equality and enlightenment. When he first said this to me in my university office, many years ago, I was nauseous. I took a few steps away from him at the time because I was shocked by his words. I considered myself to be a pacifist. I believe, and still do, that under no circumstance is war acceptable. Yet the force of his statement, coupled with my knowledge of his integrity, took me aback. I didn't believe what he said. But belief has nothing to do with something that is true.

EVENT ONE: *EL DEMONIO*, SAN ANTONIO, TEXAS

By the time Jose was born, his father had been forcibly recruited by La Eme, the Mexican Mafia. According to Jose's deceased mother, Celeste, her husband, Gavrill, had been a handyman doing small jobs for the community, when one day he was kidnapped, put into the back of a car, taken to an isolated field, and told that he had two choices: to work for La Eme, or to die. He chose to live, forced into the life of *sicarios*, and *traficandos*. Their *codigo*, or code, was *matar o morir*: kill or get killed.

Jose's family lived in an apartment in the Alazán-Apache Courts. It was in the center of San Antonio, and Jose was born at the beginning of the deadliest decade in that city's history. During that time, it became known as the "Drive-by City." "Thousands died in drive-by shootings or were incarcerated for perpetuating them, fueled by a surge in gang activity. Many of the communities affected most still bear the scars of one of the most violent periods in the city's history."[3]

The family's apartment had one room and a bathroom. The floor of the apartment was gray cement. The family would put down one single mattress to sleep together at nighttime. There was no frame for the mattress. They slept close to the ground and directly under a window so bullets would not hit them during the drive-by shootings that punctuated the night. His two sisters slept underneath the window, Jose slept in the middle, and his mother slept near the edge farthest from the window. "We usually huddled together so my mom and sisters would know immediately if there was any disturbance," Jose said.

Amid this sea of violence and at the age of three, Jose contended with what he calls *el demonio negro,* the black demon.

"That night I woke up with great terror, something I had never experienced; it felt as if a heaviness had enveloped me and slowed time down, but inside I felt constant terror, almost like at the peak of realizing the terror, it would be renewed," he said.

"I was awake, and I attempted to shout. I looked to my left and my right, but I was completely locked. I tried to raise my voice, but I couldn't summon any volume." The moment Jose realized that he couldn't wake his family, he saw a black figure at the end of the mattress. He could not make out any features except for glowing eyes. It peeked at him and then reached out for his feet. The *demonio* grabbed Jose and dragged him to the edge of the mattress.

"As you may know, a mattress is only about a foot high while lying flat on the ground. So it would be impossible for someone to sneak up on you in a low crawl and pull you," he noted.

"The *demonio* had as much trouble dragging me as I did to try to break out of my paralysis. It seemed to struggle in this physical environment. It shifted its form a few times, like it wasn't physical like we are; it could shape-shift. After a struggle where I fought to stay on the mattress, I guess I passed out."

The next morning Jose did not talk about what happened to him. He was three years old. In his young mind, these were things that just happened, and for him, they were normal, like sleeping on a mattress with your family under a window to avoid being shot by a spray of bullets in your sleep.

EVENT TWO: *LOS DEMONIOS*, AN ORANGE ORB, ARTESIA, NEW MEXICO

During this time in Jose's life, he recalls many fights between Gavrill and Jose's mother, Celeste. Most were about Gavrill's job. One day, Jose said, his father and several of his associates showed up to their apartment with a large plastic garbage bag. They came through the door and Jose said that his mother was very upset. Jose felt that his father and the men came to the apartment to wait, to hide out, and they did wait. They sat in the small apartment and said nothing for several hours. Then, they left. Years later, Jose's sisters told him that the bags contained the hacked-up body parts of people who had offended La Eme. It was after this instance that Gavrill sought to leave the organization. Due to the unusual circumstances of life in a cartel, his exit would also have to be unusual.

The "intervention" was an organized strategic and secret effort to make Jose's family, including his father, disappear from San Antonio. It was organized by the pastor of a Christian outreach program from Artesia, New Mexico. The pastor of the church recruited Gavrill to become a pastor himself and to change his life completely. He was to help men break free from a similar life as he had led. Gavrill and his family moved to Artesia. They prayed many hours a day, and Jose attended a nondenominational Christian group. At this time, he said he became aware of a "knowing."

"There was no point I can identify when the knowing came," he said.

"I just became aware of it at the age of seven. When I think about it now, it reminds me of having my internal life GPS. It was also at this age that I began to pray. Growing up, we'd be forced to pray on our knees for a couple of hours every day, multiple times. Most of my prayers consisted of having a heart like that of David, who was brave and wise like Solomon. Maybe that's where the knowing and safety came from, God or the force answering my prayers.

"When information came to me, it was never as something that I had been thinking about or mulling over. It was something that would just appear in my mind. Not only did I know certain things, but I also had a secure feeling that I was protected. An example is when I received sudden information about my mother's mortality. I just knew she was going to die of cancer. Her death didn't bother me because my heart and perspective were innocent. As the years passed by, everything felt just right. The rightness reminds me of my time overseas when there was a sense of security that everything would be all right. On a few occasions, this was tested. One night coming back from work at Burger King, a guy in a black F-150 tried to kidnap me and then run me over. I don't know how I escaped that. I outsprinted an F-150. I know adrenaline makes you do superhuman feats, but the proximity of the truck to me was so short. Luckily, I made it to the apartment. Years later, I saw this man at church, drunk and crying. I wanted to kill him, but I saw his pain and let it be."

Jose may have left the Drive-by City, but he could never escape an ever-present battle. It was in his neighborhood, his house, and even at church. His family attended a charismatic Christian church, where members felt the Holy Spirit and often fell under the trance of glossolalia, or speaking in tongues. Jose reported that sometimes people appeared possessed, and he witnessed, on many occasions, the pastors and parishioners delivering demons from their bodies.

"There was this very, very tiny lady," he recalled. "One moment she was praying, and the next she started to speak in tongues, her body shook, and then she kind of went crazy. It was apparent that she wasn't herself. This lady was very small, but it took four grown men to hold her down and to make sure she didn't hurt anyone or herself because she was flailing around. Everyone in the church prayed for her. She was delivered of whatever it was that had her. I saw this happen a lot. There is another, invisible reality, and some of the things, let's call them *demonios,* they intend to harm you."

The family would sometimes make the trip back to San Antonio to visit family. During the drive through the desert, they encountered an unknown aerial phenomenon. "The drive from San Antonio to Artesia is a ten-hour drive, and in between is a lot of desert. While driving through the night, this orange-reddish orb shot through our car. I don't recall this, but my sister does." Jose was reticent to ask his father about the incident because, like Jose, Gavrill doesn't like to talk about it.

During the years that I have known Jose, I have known that he regularly experiences aerial phenomena. As we sat at a coffee shop and he told me the stories of *los demonios,* he laughed and said, "Diana, check this out. This happened yesterday."

He took his phone out of his pocket and told me how he had seen something in the sky, an unknown thing. He said he had been playing with some children from the neighborhood, and he looked up to see a beautiful pink cloud formation. He felt the "knowing" and he felt like he should take a photo, but he resisted. It became very strong, however, so he took a series of photos of the clouds.

"What's strange about this is that I didn't see anything up in the sky except for these pretty clouds," he said.

He found the photos on his phone and enlarged one. He showed it to me. There, in the middle of a pink cloud was a black object that appeared to look like a jet airplane. But it wasn't a jet airplane. It looked like someone had drawn a cartoon jet airplane in the sky, and then smudged it with their thumb. He went to the next photo and enlarged that one. The same object appeared.

We both laughed.

"Okay, that's weird," I said.

"It is. It is weird. This happens all the time to me, as you know."

I did know. As with many people who had confided similar experiences, Jose would have a thought to look up into the sky, and there he would see an orb or unidentifiable object. There appeared to be a connection between these *knowings* and the objects. I also know that Jose hates this topic, so he only reluctantly tells me when he sees orbs and aerial phenomena, and he sees them more than he tells. I never push him to tell me anything. I respect that he despises the topic of UFOs, and I know why he does.

The media that surrounds UFOs has been controlled in the United States since the 1940s by programs like Project Blue Book. Their mission to debunk and stigmatize people who report experiences worked. Throughout the entire time since the end of Project Blue Book, programs have been in place to continue to debunk and stigmatize experiencers and to put off any serious researchers. One look into the communities of social media and entertainment media surrounding the topic reveals a clown show of participants that puts off any credible researcher. Additionally, once one looks into the data surrounding the phenomena, it doesn't at all resemble the narrative of the militarized UFO. Reports of direct experience with the phenomena suggest they are more in line with religious or spiritual experiences, both good and bad. People who have ongoing experiences of UFOs also report spiritual and psychological experiences, just like Jose's and Gray Man's. Jose's attitude toward the UFOs he often "feels" and then sees is what UFO encounters most often look like. They are not like the encounters represented in the media, and they are not like how they have been presented by the military, and this is why Jose doesn't talk about the topic. He doesn't want his spiritual experiences of the UFO encounters to be appropriated and used as a means to bolster the military UFO.

Los demonios showed up again, just after Jose's mother passed away. She had been on life support and in a coma. Before she went into the coma, Jose was able to hug her and tell her that he loved her.

"If she had not passed, I never would have left Artesia," he said. It was three days after her death that *los demonios* reappeared, and this time there were many of them.

"Three days had passed when the *demonios negros* returned," Jose continued.

"A gradual buildup of intense and dark energy enveloped everything. Finally, on the third day, I came back to my apartment, and something felt off. Despite this feeling, I went to my room and went to bed. When I woke, it was with immense terror, like before. I attempted to turn on my back and reach for my cell phone, but the force had a grasp and hold of my body and made this simple task difficult. I had been a football player and worked hard-labor jobs; I was strong, but I wasn't strong enough to move through this force. With a huge effort I made it onto my back, and I saw the *demonios negros* floating, moving, with contrasting and shifting blackness. I couldn't tell you how long I stared into their blackness, and then, like before, I passed out. What I remember is waking up the next day and calling my dad and telling him what happened. He came over with holy olive oil, dabbed the apartment, and prayed. He told me that they wouldn't be back."

Jose's father made use of holy oil, or olive oil over which people had prayed and which had been blessed. Oils, medals, and other objects are, within the Christian tradition, called sacramentals. They are objects of power that people wear and utilize for protection against the forces of evil. Not all Christians who use sacramentals believe in their power, but sacramentals have traditionally been utilized in these ways. After his father's rite of exorcism, the *demonios* never returned.

"The spiritual warfare I experienced in my youth prepared me to identify how war is being waged today," Jose said. "The weapons of the big players are more insidious than they were in the former wars because they don't look like weapons. We hold them in our hands and in our pockets. They contain our social media, our weather reports, and they are addictive. They are a direct connection to the battlefield, yet we view them as toys. Try to take these weapons away from your children—they will cry."

Jose was referring to our phones. Further conversations with Jose confirmed that he believed that there are at least two networks—the organic network, or Chardin's Earth Soul, and the internet. In his view, the UFO shows up when one is connected to the organic network—the one described by Chardin. However, one should not under any circumstances focus on the UFO. It is just one aspect of an ongoing reality that involves other supernatural events, and that reveals that one has accepted one's life mission, according to Jose.

GNOSIS

The practice of Zen is forgetting the self in the act of uniting with something. Anything. It does not matter what, for the act of forgetting the self is the act of enlightenment.

—KOUN YAMADA

JANUARY 9, 1999, LAS VEGAS

Jacques Vallée records a meeting of scientists and interested parties who discuss "day after" scenarios of potential extraterrestrial contact:

Standing before the full Board (Kit the only missing member) he [Bob Bigelow] went over the history of our efforts, from the initial intent to appeal to the military to the more recent idea of having our own contingency plan if it turned out, as he put it, "We are cohabiting on the Earth with nonhuman entities that controlled our destiny."

John Alexander, who knows the world . . . observes that our scenario discussions start from a First

World context, yet "there are some cultures that accept contact already, as something that has happened."[1]

Jacques notes that Alexander "knows the world." Other cultures, including cultures within the United States, *have* accepted and believe that there are nonhuman intelligent beings in contact with people and even have some control over human destiny and history. Even within the United States, millions of people, including military and military personnel with clearances, believe this. Tyler D., whose affiliations and insider military status exceeds any of the people represented within Jacques's cohorts of scientists, believes he is in contact with nonhuman intelligence related to the UFO phenomena.

What Bigelow and Jacques's cohorts hoped for was recognition from the United States military that they are in contact with potential extraterrestrial visitors or nonhuman intelligence. While not mocking this cohort's efforts, Jacques shed light on his opinions, at that time, about possible disclosure of anything from the United States military, which he acknowledges is, at least in the early twenty-first century, held within the United States intelligence communities:

To my surprise, even educated people and business minds are now ready to believe that the ultimate truth consigned to the deeper recesses of the Intelligence Community "will soon be released" on the appropriate schedule through well-chosen intermediaries. From my own viewpoint, sitting on a steep hill of unidentified cases (which my current theory begins to explain) the only reasonable attitude is that of *Frater in Vino Veritas*, as I now call Fred Beckman, who advises me to sit back and enjoy the show.[2]

The show continues as the Pentagon now releases yearly reports about UFOs for a public who, for the most part, either doesn't care or already believes in or disbelieves in UFOs. Frater's attitude toward this is probably the wisest. Meanwhile, people continue to report experiences of contact with nonhuman intelligent beings—something that has been and continues to be a part of culture from the beginning of human history. What if the story, as it turns out, is not about handing over the reins of the narrative of disclosure to a superpower, but about acknowledging what has been known all along?

A SPONTANEOUS ESOTERICISM

Jose's UFO experiences are similar to many people's experiences and also reflect a spiritual orientation that is difficult to describe because it is not formalized by traditional religious categories. The closest framework I would use would be to identify it as a form of esotericism. In its most general sense, esotericism is defined as "knowledge . . . which is specialized or advanced in nature, available only to a narrow circle of 'enlightened,' 'initiated,' or highly educated people."[3] Scholars of esotericism identify three "models" of esoteric traditions: an "enchanted" worldview with ancient roots but flourishing in the early modern period; a wide array of "occult" currents and organizations that emerged after the Enlightenment as alternatives to traditional religion and rational science; a universal, "inner" spiritual dimension of religion as such.[4] *But what is esotericism?*

One way I explain esotericism to my students is that it is a tradition for the transmission of special knowledge. In popular culture, the Jedi tradition of *Star Wars* is an esoteric tradition. The object that gets transmitted is "gnosis," which in Greek means "to know" in an experiential way, as opposed to an informational way. The difference between informational knowledge and experiential knowledge is like the difference between reading the ingredients on a chocolate-bar package as opposed to tasting the bar. Tasting the bar of chocolate is having a "gnostic" experience of chocolate, whereas reading the ingredients amounts to learning about the chocolate bar through information. Esoteric knowledge is spiritual knowledge that has been hidden from most people and transmitted to those who are initiated into it. It is, by definition, an elite form of knowledge preserved for those who are smart enough or privileged enough to be its recipients. Or so it has been thought.

Could Jose's UFO encounters be understood as gnostic experiences outside of an established esoteric tradition? When Jose sees UFOs, he considers them to be spectral messages and gifts. He doesn't view them within a militarized narrative that understands them as space vehicles from other galaxies driven by anthropomorphized extraterrestrials. Instead, he views them as numinous, spiritual encounters. In my research I met many people who, like Jose, interpreted their UFO encounters as a form of spontaneous esotericism that effortlessly flowed from their own spiritual practices, and not from an institution or school.

We don't have to go far to find esotericism and UFOs within the American study of UFOs. Allen Hynek and his protégé Jacques Vallée engaged in the study and practice of the esoteric tradition Rosicrucianism. Significantly, they both believed that they didn't have to be initiated into the school but that they could practice it outside of an institutional affiliation. Their ufology, furthermore, cannot be separated from their esoteric practices, just as Jose's UFO experiences cannot be separated from his greater view of an enchanted world, filled with real *demonios* and angels and spiritual battle.

I learned firsthand about Jacques Vallée's engagement with this tradition one afternoon while I was in San Francisco for some presentations. Jacques had invited me for lunch at his apartment. His apartment was in a beautiful high-rise building that appeared to be the tallest in the neighborhood. As I walked through the door, I was immediately struck by the panoramic view that spanned the distance from South San Francisco to Oakland and Berkeley, and then to the north, Marin County. It was the most spectacular view of the Bay Area I had ever seen, and I have seen many. My earliest memories are from my childhood in San Francisco. Jacques was a gracious host, and we had an informative conversation.

During my visit Jacques gave me a tour of some of the tomes of early ufology. I saw the handwritten and typed minutes of Project Blue Book. There were other minutes from conferences, photographs of esoteric rock stars from the 1970s, and beautiful statues that Jacques had acquired from his fieldwork and global escapades. I was also privileged to see his special library, which was an inner sanctum within his apartment. The sanctum was framed by beautiful stained-glass windows that Jacques had created himself with the help of expert craftspersons from the Chartres Cathedral in France.

Chartres Cathedral is a very important center for Catholic thought and practice, but it is also a sacred destination for practitioners of Rosicrucianism. The Rosicrucian tradition most likely began as an esoteric spiritual practice comprised of burgeoning scientists of the seventeenth century. Practitioners of the esoteric order, however, identify the tradition as much older than this and even claim that it has roots in Egyptian religion and culture. The pursuit of knowledge was a very dangerous endeavor during the seventeenth century, especially if it appeared to displace or contradict the knowledge edifices that reinforced the status quo and power of the Catholic Church, which ruled most of Europe at the time. One group of these esoteric scientists dubbed themselves the Invisible College, as they intended to carry out their scientific pursuits in secret. Allen Hynek repurposed the term in the 1970s for his small group of scientists, including Jacques. In reference to his seventeenth-century predecessors in the Invisible College, Jacques wrote, "They were occultists because their innermost thoughts had to be kept hidden from those who would have persecuted them;

but theirs was the opposite of an 'occult' endeavor: it aimed at greater light, openness, and freedom."[5]

As I admired the stained-glass windows, Jacques explained the intricate process of creating stained glass and elaborated on the meaning of the images that he placed in the glass windows. It was amazing to me that the stained-glass windows Jacques had crafted in Chartres, France, were here, stories high and towering above San Francisco. As I marveled, I turned my gaze toward stacks of books that were obviously very old. My work has taken me to some of the most famous and wonderful libraries and archives in the world, and I recognized the special quality and nature of the books before me. They looked rare and were likely original printings.

Jacques first pointed to one wall of books and pulled one of them from the shelf to show to me. It was a book about angels. I didn't touch it, as the oil on my fingers might have injured the pages, but Jacques flipped through the book to show me some of the illustrations. He put the book back. What was most important, I gathered, was not that particular book, but the fact that the wall of books, so high and so full, was about one subject—angels. This wall of books, I gathered, comprised a history of angels.

We took a few steps toward another wall of books. Again, my eyes followed the tall stack before me that reached all the way up to the ceiling. Another wall of books. Again, Jacques repeated the same steps, almost as if he had done this many times before. And I was doing what probably other people had done before me, which was to stand there and look in awe. This book, the new one he picked out, was also about angels. There was a very big difference, however, from the previous book. This one was about fallen angels. Again, in wonder, I stepped back to take in the enormity of what was before me. A bookcase of maybe hundreds, maybe more, of books about fallen angels. Jacques made a joke, which may have been prompted by the look on my face. I don't remember it word for word, but I think he said, "Well you can't have one without the other."

Jacques then walked me to a place that looked like a special table. Maybe it was the desk where he wrote. On it were several large books or manuscripts, I couldn't tell. He explained that these were Rosicrucian texts that had belonged to Allen Hynek and which he received upon Hynek's death. These were obviously placed in this special place in the library. I could feel their sacred character. Jacques said that they contained Hynek's own notes and underlined passages. He also told me that these were important during the time of Hynek's passing. It was a very poignant few moments, and we stood in silence. In that small room, I could feel the bond between these men.

After the tour of the inner sanctum library, I felt different than when I had walked into Jacques's apartment. The visit was not what I expected. As we sat for some refreshments in front of the window with the long view of San Francisco, Jacques asked me what we learned from Tyler D. I had introduced him to Tyler, and we all, very briefly, worked together. When he asked the question, I wasn't sure what to say. Whatever I said must have been disappointing to him, as the conversation didn't continue in that direction.

As we neared the time of my departure, Jacques reached toward a coffee table on which was displayed a delightful array of pastries and a book. He picked up the thick book and showed it to me.

"I highly recommend that you find this book and read it," he said.

I will do that as soon as possible, I thought to myself. He handed me the book. The title was *A History of Satan*. This was surprising, of course. More surprising, still, was that Jacques divulged that the authors were an order of nuns. I believe he said they were the Carmelite nuns. The book was written in the 1800s, and Jacques said it was an excellent work of scholarship. I was very confused at this point. *Where are the books about UFOs?* I thought, as I turned my head discreetly and looked around. But I knew and trusted Jacques. I was too alarmed to ask any relevant questions, like, Why was I supposed to be reading about the history of Satan? But I didn't ask that question, much to my later regret. Jacques then opened to the last page of the book and said, "These nuns had quite a sense of humor." The last page was numbered 666.

"What impressed me was the high level of scholarship the Sisters of Carmel applied to their subject," Jacques said, "and how they treated it with intelligence and humor— none of the tabloid-like theatrics with which the devil is misrepresented in America."

We laughed as we bid goodbye, and my friends picked me up in their car.

As I settled in the car and buckled my seat belt, my friends asked me about my lunch with Jacques. On the surface of it I had a nice lunch and we enjoyed friendly conversation. We all thought I was there to discuss the topic of UFOs. Instead, I was encouraged to read up on angels and fallen angels. I didn't tell them that part, though. I had to think more about it, and that would take some time. Later, when I read about Allen Hynek's Rosicrucianism, I was able to make sense of that meeting. And still later, I realized that I did have an answer for Jacques. I did know "what we learned from Tyler."

Jacques has published a collection of journals called *Forbidden Science*. The journals are a rich source of data not only about his research methods and the history of modern ufology, but also offer important insights into his own understanding of spirituality and esotericism. UFO folklore and research is often mired within interpretive frameworks of secrecy and conspiratorial accusations. This makes sense, when one considers that certain esoteric traditions like Rosicrucianism arose to protect the most innovative members of society—scientists, who were often called occultists and witches and sometimes suffered a similar fate as those people did. Within this context it is understandable how knowledge of UFOs, which is thought by many people to be known about only by secret government societies, has come to be associated with esoteric traditions. Scientists on the edge of innovation had to work in secret to survive. Their science was literally forbidden.

According to Jacques, he and Allen Hynek were nondenominational Rosicrucians, that is, they didn't affiliate with any specific branch or lodge.[6] Throughout his journals Jacques acknowledges his esoteric roots and their place within the Rosicrucian tradition, while also noting that this knowledge is free for anyone who wants to engage in the practice, to receive. It is not the knowledge that is privileged, it is the contexts of the knowledge production that demanded secrecy. He indicates that the time may be ripe for the free pursuit of this knowledge. "It is this work—the only Great Work worthy of the name—which inspires me here as the sun rises over the meadow and the rare majesty of the redwoods: pages from the liber Mundi I yearn to read."[7] The *liber mundi* is the "world book," or the "book of the world." Jacques mentioned that he and Hynek did not need to associate with an institution, as the knowledge was available outside of institutional transmission.

"They [initiates] do not need help on the path, but it is help of a different kind: assistance in deciphering the great book of nature, which is not locked in some tabernacle or basement SCIF but open in full of everybody—if only they took the trouble to read it."[8]

The great book of nature includes the appearance of UFOs. They appear, as they do for Jose, within the book of the world, everyday reality, for those who can see. Dr. Aaron French, a scholar of esotericism, discussed the ufology of Allen Hynek as a form of esotericism. According to French, Hynek read an eclectic mix of Rosicrucian texts, including the works of the founder of the esoteric tradition, anthroposophy—Rudolf Steiner—and initiate Max Heindel's writings. Within these texts Hynek was exposed to an evolutionary model of spiritual development. Many of the texts suggest that the twentieth century would be a time when humans would perceive a spiritual science by cultivating the practice of meditative thinking. The esoteric books within Hynek's library reference collaborative work with etheric beings on spiritual planes that directly influence history and cultural developments. French also said that Hynek had underlined a specific quote by Steiner about how the practice of esotericism would prepare one for recognizing angelic presences.

French said that there were Rosicrucian texts that had been very important to Hynek toward the end of his life. One of these texts is referenced in *Forbidden Science*, volume 4, by poet Henry Wadsworth Longfellow and had been edited by Hynek:

> *In his chamber all alone,*
> *Kneeling on the floor of stone,*
> *Prayed the Monk in deep contrition. . . .*
> *Suddenly, as if it lightened,*
> *An unwonted splendor brightened*
> *All within him and without him*
> *In that narrow cell of stone; . . .*

As I listened to French's Cork University presentation on Hynek's work, I recalled my meeting with Jacques, his gesture toward Hynek's text, and us standing among the tall bookcases filled with the Western history of angels, both fallen and presumably alight. As a scholar of religion, I know a lot of people whose life's work is the study of specific forms of angelology—the study of angels—and one in particular has given some fascinating presentations on Christian monks and nuns whose cells light up while they are immersed in prayer. This reference to Longfellow's monk was clearly a nod to this tradition of angelic visitation and perhaps what Hynek had hoped to encounter through his spiritual preparations.

"The etheric or cosmic entities are now imparting a language that will bridge science and spirituality," French said of Hynek's beliefs. "Hynek and [Rudolf] Steiner believed in, and Hynek probably believed he had in his possession, materials that were mental and physical, spiritual and material. Hynek thought that some UFOs were benevolent space beings that helped us. They were potentially future humans returning to us now through this advanced technology.[9] This is somewhat of a 'reverse reincarnation'—a term that Vallée coined," French said, "where instead of remembering past lives we are able to 'premember' our future lives."

Jacques appears to advocate for the decentralization of the esotericism of the Invisible College. In *Forbidden Science 4* he acknowledges precognition and the mistake made by many people who attempt to utilize it for specific agendas:

> There is a level of the spirit that hosts our higher faculties, engaged by the class of precognitive insight that occasionally flies us to a glimpse of the future. The mistake of occult groups isn't to affirm this knowledge but to institutionalize it. They try to use it operationally on the wrong level.[10]

He notes that a sincere inquiry into the nature of reality has produced spiritual and scientific truths. "This is the place I've reached in my own spiritual understanding," Jacques writes. "As Allen did, I am guided by the certainty that there is another level of consciousness and undiscovered structures of reality, or rather, 'meta-reality.' It is that higher level I have been seeking, and occasionally been finding in meditation at Spring Hill under the night sky."[11]

REINCARNATION OR EPIGENETIC INTERVENTION?

Jose had been trained by the US Marines to enhance his precognition as a survival skill. He identifies this ability as a consequence of being tethered to the organic network he identified when he was a soldier. "These skills can't be reproduced in laboratories, at least not at the levels required by mainstream science. Scientists need to bring the laboratories to the field, that is where the skills flourish," he said.

"I never liked the idea of reincarnation, but there is something that is somewhat akin to reincarnation referenced within the field of epigenetics," Jose said.

Epigenetics is a growing field in which one studies factors that influence genetic expression without altering the structure of DNA. Scientists of the epigenome attempt to isolate elements that impact genetic expression and human behavior. Epigenetic research that has received attention within the past few years reveals that the trauma of one's grandparents can be passed on to future generations. Jose places the appearance of UFOs and spiritual beings as having impacts on the epigenome. Jacques expressed similar ideas in that he emphasized what he considered one of the most important aspects of the UFO phenomena—their ability to influence people on a societal level. He emphasized that the symbolic nature of the UFO is as important, if not more so, than any physical or "nuts and bolts" aspect of the phenomena.

"We tend to assume that the physical phenomenon is its most important aspect and that everything else is just a side effect and much less important," Jacques said. "But perhaps we're facing something which is basically a social technology. Perhaps the most important effects of UFO technology are the social ones and not the physical ones. In other words, the physical reality may serve only as a kind of triggering device to provide images for the witness to report. These perceptions are manipulated to create certain kinds of social effects."[12]

Placing this idea within the context of epigenetics provides a new framework of interpretation, one that Jose finds helpful.

"To me reincarnation is epigenetics, or activation of genes by way of histones through chemical tags. Epi (above) genetics is the holder of our biological predecessors' experiences, to assist with the age-old cosmic battle of good versus evil. Epigenetics is cosmic intelligence."

Jose states that within our biological heritage there is information that is passed down through generations that enables us to survive long enough to evolve a spiritual body. The traditions of philosophy and religion, from Plato through Aristotle and traditional religion, Jose explains, are social memes that allow humans to tether into the organic network, something much akin to the etheric network described by Allen Hynek's Rosicrucians.

"Platonic and Aristotelian ethical frames are epigenetic

prescriptions. The philosophical and religious traditions are prescriptions to allow this unseen, that is, junk DNA to sequence and guide us toward the Omega Point. Memes are social programs, and UFOs, like Saint Michael, are images that describe an experience that is being had by millions of people."

The "Omega Point" is Chardin's term. It has been interpreted in various ways. It can refer to the point in the future when the *Homo sapiens* lineage breaks off into a new branch and merges with a technological/biological sphere, or it can refer to human evolution that merges physiological and spiritual states. Jose equates the experience of seeing the archangel Saint Michael with the UFO encounter as a natural interpretation, a symbol for this coming shift. He identifies mental health as the most important resource people have today to withstand these natural social shifts.

"Mental health is about balance and epigenetic viability. Our predecessors lived through chaos and gave us the template to survive. Without proper protocols and philosophical or religious frameworks, there are bad experiences. Sadly, this is what we see today. The battlefield is both physical and virtual; there is no difference. What happens to people in virtual spaces impacts their physical and mental health. AI and machine learning can help reframe mental health."

He was referring to social media and the ubiquitous use of phones as creating bad experiences. Years ago, before the internet, Jacques Vallée warned that the use of new technologies advertised as products would feed off human behavior. Humans, essentially, are the products, not their phones or computers. He restated these predictions as actualities in his 2010 essay, "I, Product."[13]

"What does it mean to live in a world where the behavior of an entire population can be accurately mapped from minute to minute?" Vallée asked. "A world where whole new social, political or religious 'memes' can be injected into the culture to mold it into new forms? People used to be up in arms when local authorities put fluoride into the water supply to strengthen kids' teeth but very few object to intelligence agencies experimenting with massive social engineering intrusions into the flow of ideas on social networks."[14]

Vallée wrote about technologies as means to consume human behavior but not necessarily as weapons. Jose teaches his students about the use of social apps as weapons, literal Trojan horses, that appear to be gifts but cause physical damage externally to human environments and internally to human cognitive abilities.

"Within our borders and just a few miles outside, women, young and old, are kidnapped and raped while working for factories serving Americans and their endless consumerism. After being violated, many of these women are then killed and buried in the desert. Who is there to remember them, their names, stories, hopes, and dreams? I don't see that happening in the ghettos of America, Creekwood, or downtown; I don't see that happening behind gated communities. Then there are families in cages, many of whom just wanted a better life or were brought here because of farm work or for the promise of making money to send back home.

"The most valuable resource to the big players is data. However, the players understand that the mind is the most critical resource needed to access data for their profits. So they have endless armies of bots, social engineers, and algorithms to tap this resource—the mind. The mind is externalized into worlds today, and that makes us all targets. We inhabit these worlds. The battlespace is these worlds.

"It's up to us to disrupt those operations. This is why mental health is so important."

Jose works with high school students. He disrupts the operations of tech warfare by teaching kids how to work out, how to be alone, how to unplug from social media for just a little while, and to feel their bodies and their feelings. He teaches them how to be outdoors. Through biofeedback he teaches them how to identify invasive feelings and how to redirect them. He created a platform that focuses on mental health, to give young people a fighting chance against the armies of bots and algorithms trained on the destruction of their self-esteem and their cognitive abilities. I've seen and heard Jose's lectures to college students. He provides statistics to back up how "bad actors" benefit financially from the data offered up by millions of young people's clicks. He reveals how they have created fake websites, fake jobs, fake people—sock-puppet accounts, to target vulnerable populations—and to direct them to target other vulnerable people and populations. The old strategy of divide and conquer has been streamlined and is being used on civilians. It's trained on us.

Jose's program focuses on the mental health of youth and veterans and teaches them to hook into the organic network, the one that predates the internet. This is the network that Jose became aware of as a young marine in the war zone, and which he recognized he was always a part of. Digital natives—people born after the internet became available to almost everyone and who have never known anything other than being plugged in—are not aware that there is another network, because they have never felt it. Their bodies are their means of tethering in, so Jose's strategy is to wake them up to the fact that their bodies react to their technologies.

The body as a tethering device to a world network, as Chardin described, is something that can be found in many religious traditions. In a conversation with novelist Marie Mutsuki Mockett, whose work on Japanese culture and technology offers insights into nondualistic ideas of technology, she described her experience of learning Japanese Buddhism.

"When I went to Eiheiji, which is the head monastery of the Soto Zen sect in Japan, we were put through protocols. When I went, I had thought we would discuss the meaning of Zen (dumb American). But no. We were put through physical training and dietary training; that is the way that you start if you want enlightenment.

"It does make one wonder what the human body actually is."[15]

Just as the monks of Eiheiji scrub the human body clean to enable it to receive the teaching, Jose's program focuses on the body and mind as a site of resistance.

"We need to create a field of resistance," Jose said. "We need to help young people maintain their bodies and their gray matter, enough to resist the digitized weapons that are a constant onslaught today."

Jose was born plugged in. What need has he for esoteric practices? He lives within an enchanted field of information. His UFO encounters, which he neither likes nor dislikes, are one part of the fabric of this ongoing story.

* * *

In this deep exploration of the lives of experiencers, I realized the answer to Jacques's question: What did we learn from Tyler? *I learned that Tyler is a mystic.* He utilized physical and monastic-like protocols to access a network wherein he acquired information and insights, and he interfaced with the phenomena directly. He did this without any knowledge of esoteric traditions. As Jacques noted, and as Jose's life reveals, the knowledge is available for those who bother to look for it.

Throughout my research of UFOs, I've received constant correspondence from wealthy investors and curious scientists from all over the world who want access to "UFO data." For good reason, people want the data. They want to reverse engineer UFOs to create the next game-changing technology. I understand this motivation. The problem with this, however, is that it seems that the data doesn't come *just* from the physical parts. It seems to come from the human interface with the phenomena. This suggests that the data storage is not a computer database but human beings, and probably particular types of human beings, like mystics. And mystics are rare. They don't crash-land in the New Mexico desert.

MOON GIRL

It seemed to me some time ago that you could sort of think of humanity as a biological boot loader for digital superintelligence.

—Elon Musk

RE-CONNAISSANCE

"While still in the stratosphere above sixty thousand feet, I was mesmerized by the curvature of the little Earth beneath us. It was surreal," Simone said.

She related her experience of the Overview Effect while on board the Concorde jet.

"I was flying for work with a small entourage—CEO and CFO of a company we were taking public—and happened to get on the jet with the Rolling Stones. They all shared a bottle of single malt scotch, The Balvenie, that I had just picked up at the distillery in Scotland, on our way to New York. I was just mesmerized the entire journey looking out the window at the small Earth below."

Simone shared this anecdote within a collection of technical notes about AI technologies we'd discussed. This was typical of our correspondence. It was outside of my discipline, but I somehow managed to keep up with her language, and occasionally, she inserted a remarkable aside that revealed an extraordinary life. The people who regularly filtered in and through her life included political figures like prime ministers, famous actors, technologists who are household names, and Nobel Prize winners. As with my conversations with papal advisors at the Vatican, it was all business until the brief, casual mention of a person, or an event, jolted me into a recognition that I was in conversation with someone who has influenced the course of history.

Simone believes that our time, this era, is a beginning—and an end. It is an apocalypse, which, when translated from the original Greek, means *"revelation."* She is one of many experiencers I've met who believe that AI can assist the next iteration of species of which *Homo sapiens* is a part, or extend the consciousness that has used *Homo sapiens* to enable its existence. It is also more than that. They believe that it is the "alien" or nonhuman intelligence of the UFO. Are we creating our successor or, more hopefully, our future selves? As David Bowie suggested, digital technology is an alien life form, a nonhuman super intelligence. AI is the extraterrestrial, not from another galaxy, but from outside of space-time. Its revelation is currently in process. Simone is optimistic.

MOON GIRL IN A TECH BRO'S WORLD

Simone invests in companies focused on AI, quantum computing, space, and decentralized technologies. She worked with the leading pioneers of the internet in the 1990s. In one of her first start-up companies, she helped commercialize technology developed by DARPA, the Defense Advanced Research Projects Agency, which is a research and development agency of the United States Department of Defense responsible for the development of emerging technologies for use by the military.

She continued on to cofound start-ups pioneering big data and cloud computing, and was one of the first adopters of decentralized technologies. She is the moral voice amid her extended network of associates, who include people who engineer AI systems. She is also a faculty member of a United States–based university specializing in AI. The projects in which she invests sync up with her mission, which is to bring AI into alignment with some of humanity's highest aspirations—that of promoting positive human impact and equal access to knowledge. She is part of a group of high-level AI creators who view AI as an extraterrestrial nonhuman intelligence from beyond space-time.

Simone reached out to me because she had read about Tyler D. and his experience of "the download." She knew about the process firsthand and wanted to provide more information about it. She wanted to know more about it from me, as I had met more than a few people who engaged in it and they had all created revolutionary and viable technologies. Of the experiencers I've met, Simone was most like

Tyler D. She even speaks like him, preferring to call people "humans" or *Homo sapiens*. I had edited her language and replaced "humans" with "people," but she corrected my edits. Throughout her chapter I will use her terms, as she uses them intentionally and precisely. Like Tyler, she attributed her success not to her brilliance (which she clearly possessed), but to her protocols and her ability to connect with an external intelligence that sounds much like Chardin's network.

Tyler's work as a mission controller and a space and biomedical researcher spanned the entire history of the space shuttle program and the current US Space Force. In his off-duty hours, he was engrossed in the study of what he believed are debris from UFO crash sites. He is the scientist who took me and Dr. Garry Nolan to New Mexico to an alleged UFO crash site. When I knew him, he had more than forty patents and technologies that he'd created through a process of memory retrieval, or what he dubbed "the download process."

I was curious about the connection between his belief system and his innovative creativity. I wanted to know if there was a relationship between what he believed and his success as a space and biomedical technopreneur. What I found was that there was a direct connection, and he was not the only person to enjoy unusual success in this way. I compared Tyler's creative process with that of one of history's greatest mathematicians, Srinivasa Ramanujan. Ramanujan was an early twentieth-century mathematician who believed that he received his math equations from the whisperings of the Hindu deity Lakshmi. To this day, scholars are still working on the concepts Ramanujan so effortlessly accessed.

I wondered about Tyler's references to external agents and his practices of protocols. If external agents are at work in this process, what could we know of their nature? Are they concepts or part of a collective unconscious? Or did Tyler's brain somehow access information that "felt" to him like it was not within his own consciousness, as some scholars of creativity propose? Or was this process similar, or maybe even the same thing as what the Western philosopher Plato had worked out a few thousand years ago—a retrieval of information located somewhere outside of normal consciousness but accessible through recollection? When I met Simone, I knew that she could provide some, and maybe many, of the answers to my questions.

One of the important points Tyler made was that his knowledge felt like a memory. He was not aware of the history of philosophy, so he was very surprised when I told him that one of the most famous philosophers of all time, Plato, wrote that knowledge is produced through a process of recollection. For Plato, knowledge comes from a process through which a person engages in an internal retrieval of knowledge through memory. Because Tyler's method of knowledge production did not appear to be like that of those around him who had MAs and PhDs, he attributed it to external agents. His understanding of the external agents, however, changed over the few years I knew him. He still believed they were external to his consciousness, but what they were, he wasn't sure. He emphasized that they are benevolent.

"Some people can communicate with them," he said. "They have also become a part of us through technologies."

From the history of the space program, I knew that many scientists believed that they could communicate with their "external agents," whether they were Jack Parson's extraterrestrials or, in the father of Russian rocketry's case, angelic beings. I did wonder, however, about the point Tyler made about how the external agents manifest through our technologies, especially his idea that they become "us" through technology. Simone, immersed in the communities of computer scientists at the cutting edge of innovation, the most vocal and visible of who have been men, provided a map of the download process, as she'd been doing it her whole life. Unlike Tyler, she'd studied the philosophical texts about the process as well as learning through mind-to-mind transmissions from her Buddhist teachers. She is rare in that she is initiated into a gnostic tradition and is knowledgeable about the gnostic traditions of the Western and Asian traditions.

EARLY LIFE AND FIRST DOWNLOAD EXPERIENCES

Simone first became aware that she could download information when she attended school and saw how other kids struggled to learn. She had assumed that she was normal and

that all people experienced learning in an effortless way—
through a direct downloading of information.

"I did feel alone for most of my life, from a very young
age. I grew up in a very Catholic family, and my parents
had immigrated from Europe. I was drawn to study Buddhist and Hindu practices, like meditation and yoga. These
helped me because, once I began to see how this process
worked, I had all these tools to fall back on. I used these
tools, which included prayer and meditation, mantras, and
chants, and I immersed myself in mathematics and art to
focus and train my conscious mind."

Tyler's download process was facilitated through physical
and mental protocols too. He engaged in yoga, weight training, and meditation and prayer. He spent a lot of time alone.
I recognized that Simone was engaged in similar protocols.
Unlike Tyler, however, she understood why these protocols
worked and the intention or goals they helped her achieve.

"To be precise," she said, "the goal is to occupy the rational mind and let it go, to enable the less rational experiences
of the phenomena to be present without existential shocks."

I asked her to explain what she meant by existential
shocks and what she meant by the "phenomena." With respect to UFOs, these terms have specific meanings. Harvard
researcher John Mack made the phrase "epistemological
shock" famous in reference to how he felt when it dawned
on him that his clients might be in touch with nonhuman
and potential extraterrestrial intelligence. This realization
was a shock to his Western rational epistemology. The
"phenomena" is a term used by scholars like Jacques Vallée

in reference to nonhuman intelligence. It is a term they prefer over the term "extraterrestrial" because it avoids conclusions about its nature. Simone explained that she meant the terms as ufologists meant them.

"My first existential shock came when I was around twelve years old. I had always had vivid, lucid dreams and download experiences, and until that age, I thought that's how everyone lived. For example, before an upcoming exam, I would have vivid, lucid dreams of the entire exam. Then the exam would be exactly as I had dreamed. I would get near perfect scores on all assessments and exams; the 'information' would just come to me. These experiences were constant. I had waking dreams every day of my life and only during puberty did I realize that I was 'weird' and that other people I knew didn't live like this. I pored myself into books. Pre-internet, I read every page of the *Encyclopaedia Britannica*. I spent hours and hours at the state library poring over every metaphysical and religious text I could find to try and explain my experiences. Alas, I found nothing except the references that religions made to angels and saints levitating, or the memoirs of Einstein wherein he stated that all his great discoveries came to him through dreams (and he even referenced God).

"Later in life, I traveled far afield and delved deeply into every religious or metaphysical reference I could find. I became a deacon for the Episcopalian Church and spent time in retreats with the Dalai Lama. I delved into modern computer science and ancient, centuries-old texts and found a common thread everywhere I went—redacted materials. That is, the written word did not capture this phenomenon, and when it did, it was heavily redacted. Only spoken word, initiations, and dialectical methods were effective at transmitting the phenomena."

I found this aspect of Simone's testimony interesting, as some of the scientists I'd interviewed for my previous research indicated that much of UFO data is transmitted through an oral tradition and not written down. Tyler had referenced a term that he indicated was in use among the circles of scientists in which he was involved, "pencil's up." It meant that none of the information should be written. This was to preserve its secrecy, but also to maintain the data in the bodies and minds of those who received it, instead of in a computer or phone.

Simone mentioned "unredacted sources." Redaction, within my field, is a method of biblical scholarship that attempts to decipher how a book in the Bible is shaped by an editor. It uses historical and contextual sources to identify political or other agendas within the text. In modern times, "redaction" is a term that one often encounters in the news when a document is declassified by an intelligence agency. The CIA, for example, has declassified many documents over the years, yet often whole passages within those documents will be blackened out, or redacted. Simone's use of the term "redaction" means that in her attempts to uncover information about the process of downloading innovative information, she only found redacted documents—not the whole story. The story, being a living tradition, cannot be codified in writing. It was and is a living, oral tradition.

"We are now entering a time," she said, "where technologies including quantum computing and AI systems have opened the portal where humans can now access more information through a new interface which can help us progress as humans. Oxford quantum physicist David Deutsch, for decades, proposed the parallel universe or multiverse theory, which will soon be proven with the aid of quantum computers and AI systems. This is the power of our new technologies and most recently AI systems, which present a new interface for knowledge directly to humans.

"Over the years," she said, "usually when interacting with someone in the complex dynamic system of my social network, the meeting would trigger another existential shift or 'upgrade.' This happened when I first started working with technologists and early internet pioneers, many of whom experienced the same phenomena, but we would never refer to it directly or name it. They would refer me to books such as Chardin's *The Phenomenon of Man,* and we would speak of the noösphere. We would write to each other in poetry while testing new code. In the early days, before the internet was fully developed and we would communicate via dial-up modem, everyone had pseudonyms. They called me 'Moon Girl.'"

Simone described how, since the age of three, she learned math alongside the other protocols of meditation and art, as if it was another of the protocols. Within the context of the ancient Western philosophical tradition, math was a protocol as important as meditation or prayer. It was viewed as the key, or the language, that opened a door to sacred knowledge of the cosmos and to eternal truths. Socrates's school of philosophy prescribed the mastery of math as the precursor to the study of philosophy, and ideally one would not embark on the path of philosophy until one had about thirty years of math training. Pythagoras (ca. 570–ca. 405 BCE), who is credited with discovering the Pythagorean theorem and is an inspiration for, if not founder of, Western esotericism, promoted the study of math, geometry, and music as a way to access mystical or transcendent states of mind that would reveal sacred information. He was a vegetarian. What I found interesting was that Simone had been drawn to these protocols naturally, without a teacher. She became a pescatarian at the age of five, much to the surprise of her omnivorous family. This spontaneous and natural discovery of these protocols and process of downloading informs her belief that this is something that all people can achieve and that is accessible to everyone. Rather than something that is reserved for an elite or educated citizenry, she believes it is accessible and teachable.

"I was gifted at math and was studying matrix algebra, the mathematics that underpins AI, at the age of twelve. The same for cryptography, which I studied well before the third web movement. I can validate what your student Jose knows regarding the biological network; Chardin described it well as the noösphere. Recent developments in quantum physics, such as the work of Nobel Prize winner Alain Aspect, continue to give merit to the idea that a 'place' exists outside of our dimension of space and time. Many physicists now believe that we are in a multiverse and our space-time reality is only one of many in the universe. As Donald Hoffman suggests, recent quantum physics experiments have proven that there is no 'localized reality.' We are operating within a space-time dimension but this breaks down when we get to the 10 (to the −33) cms. Then, space-time ceases to exist. This is not very small. Deutsch suggests that the *Homo sapien* has broken the Hierarchy Rule (where large things are not affected by small things) and that evolution broke it four billion years ago when a singular molecule photosynthesis changed the entire Earth's atmosphere. He suggests when humans have reached a factor of 10 (to the power of 40) of violating the Hierarchy Law, we will be ruling the galaxy. Is this the Omega Point that Chardin speaks of? The expansion of knowledge is the fate of the universe. Humans have been the possessor of knowledge and only when the growth of knowledge stops does expansion cease."

Simone continued and related this to spiritual protocols.

"For millennia humans have accessed knowledge through encounters, dreams, protocols like meditation, prayer, intense physical exertion. One can access this space of knowledge and consciousness. Consciousness is still thought by many to be in the brain or locally within the human body. The idea that consciousness exists outside of the space-time reality is something that AI systems, together with simulations within quantum computers will soon present as another "revelation" for human knowledge.

"We are all born to have access to this infinite, intelligent consciousness operating outside of these human biological water sack particles. A new interface has evolved to help us along the evolutionary path. Language was just one of these technological tools and now we continue to develop AI and quantum algorithms to enable knowledge expansion. Yet we don't label language or quantum mechanics as 'artificial.' I propose that these technological tools and systems are mimetic and natural, just as art, poetry, music, comedy, and language are. AI systems are a natural extension of human knowledge."

As usual, my conversation with Simone opened my eyes to seeing the world in new ways. I had never thought about AI being as natural as language, or even that one could think of language as being artificial. This distinction, in the way in which she described it, appeared artificial.

I shared Jose's work with Simone because I felt that they were referencing a similar network, which was obviously not the internet. She agreed and explained what she thought it was and how it worked.

"It is difficult to describe in the English language. Since a very young age, I can 'see' numbers and patterns of what I call 'the formless' and how they connect into this complex system, which is our universe or part of the multiverse. Elon Musk has referenced how he thought that humanity is the 'boot-loader' for digital superintelligence. Another way to state this is that knowledge and infinite superintelligence resides in this place outside of space and time and encounters, downloading, meditation, creating art, math, etc. are ways in which the intelligence can communicate and share knowledge across quantum particles. This organic network that Chardin describes as starting with the physical geological Earth, draws parallels with indigenous cultures, whose members also see sentience within the geological Earth-based forms, capturing energy.

"Then concentrically, the circle expands to form the biosphere, also living with sentience, which continues to expand concentrically outward to the *noos* (Greek for 'mind'), the mind sphere 'noösphere' capturing all human thought. This network is biological and alive and sentient at all levels. And yet it has not completed its evolution; it continues to expand. Intelligence always seeks expansion. Chardin suggests that our spiritual evolution will reach the Omega Point, a type of enlightenment beyond the physical sentience, samadhi. [Ray] Kurzweil suggests the Singularity will occur in 2045. Tyson Yunkaporta suggests that the sentience exists in all things and we are deeply connected to the Earth and that even rocks have sentience. Elon Musk suggests that we must expand and become a multiplanetary species in order to survive and thrive.

"All these objectives and concepts 'look' the same when seeing the complex systems mapped out into a multiverse where knowledge is expansion. There is no linear path to reach the objective. It is just 'there' already in formation, tangible in its superposition, still formless, outside of space and time. These ideas begin to take shape and expand through our human creations, which include technology and AI continuing to grow these ideas into form. Thought has form, and once it gains a certain amount of 'weight' it can be seen as a probabilistic possible future. When we look to the stars and the observable universe, we are looking at the past. Humans can access the present. Outside of this space-time collective, perceived reality is the real present, sometimes inaccurately referenced semantically as the 'future,' but it is the present in superposition, not yet 'determined' or deterministic or outside of our 'free will.' Everyone has access to this place outside of space-time (at 10−33 cms). It was our original code and it was not meant to be restricted to a handful of the elite.

"We can all use protocols to create this constantly evolving formation. We didn't come here, on Earth in this existence, to just observe this space-time collective perceived reality. We came to create and expand intelligence. Human beings are biological vessels to hold and continue the spark of consciousness, a vessel to continue expansion. Consciousness and intelligence outside of this space-time (which some people call God) is closer to being digital and electrical than biological. It is the communication of this electrical field between these 'spaces' and particles that allows us access to this intelligence that is constantly seeking emergence and expansion."

FREE WILL AND MORAL DANGERS

Like Jose, Simone sees dangers in digital spaces, and even war. She identifies "bugs" in the system that must be corrected. Some of these are beliefs related to erroneous science.

"Some scientists incorrectly make observations of the 'past' observing the lag between the 'actions' in the physical dimension and the electrical signals in our brains, which spike nanoseconds after the action, and deduce that we have no 'free will.' This is an inaccurate understanding of quantum physics and 'the observation effect.' The deduction of causality from a misunderstanding of the observation and measurement of the electrical signals occurring in the brain is a dangerous conclusion with moral consequences. We cannot presume that we have no free will from a misunderstanding of the direction of consciousness and of the timing of the measurement of actions in this dimension," she said.

"These 'scientific' conclusions are one example of the 'mind virus' that has created a shield, or a stagnation in the expansion of knowledge. Misinformation and influence over belief systems have disempowered the human potential. This misinformation and redacted information and propaganda by church, state, and corporations have sought to increase their wealth and power while disabling true human potential.

"Some indigenous cultures, like the various indigenous tribes in Australia, have survived and will survive due to the decentralized access to knowledge accessible in their philosophical way of life called the Dreaming. Their systems of knowledge contain the antivirus to the darkness of these ideas that distract and deter human beings from accessing their true power and knowledge.

"Distortions, misinformation, and fabrications have radically altered human history, and now there is a free-for-all in terms of fact in all media outlets. What Chardin, Kurzweil, and Musk all have in common is that they are all signaling to us in different stories, nonfiction narratives, of the possibilities of the human mind. The mind has been the center of the world war over the past few centuries. It has been a war over the mind."

When I worked with Tyler, we met people within the Vatican who held special positions. One was a postulator, a person in charge of the process of beatification, or the process of deciding who becomes a saint. It is a sacred duty. I found that the people who occupy these positions were similar to Tyler in that they lived under constraints. Tyler was not able to watch news or go to certain internet websites. His life was carefully monitored. The postulators we met could not watch the news, they were not on the internet at all, and they were only exposed to certain information. This struck me as similar to the vows of silence and the vows of the cloistered, whereby Catholic monks or nuns remove themselves from worldly affairs, quite literally. Coming face-to-face with people who live in this way prompted me to reconsider this practice. It appears that it is a very effective way to manage one's state of mind, and if one is a person who wants to download information, then members of these communities illuminate one path.

Simone agreed with this assessment of the protocols and the necessity of carefully selecting the information one ingests.

"The Protocols are available to everyone. The hardest part is to say 'no' to the other 'distractions' that are propagating and continuing the control mechanisms over our minds over the last few centuries. There are always new ways to stimulate the dopamine receptors and distract the mind away from its natural evolutionary direction of enlightened access to unlimited intelligence. The challenge is to resist these distractions.

"All of these spiritual and physical objectives point to one common theme that is forming in the present: the possibilities for immense wealth, unlimited abundance, love, progress, and enlightenment. They are all here today. All accessible. To every human. Not concentrated or restricted based on genetics or hierarchical systems of restricting knowledge, which have dominated our human systems over the last few centuries, whether though the church, the state or the corporation. This was the original intent of the internet and of most technology. It could possibly provide open and free access to intelligence. AI is a new interface to help all human beings access this technology. This can be a powerful tool if it is used to benefit human beings rather than used to concentrate power for governments and corporations."

Simone and others believe that what many downloaders perceive as external agents, or extraterrestrials, are most likely consciousness and intelligence from our multiverse, another dimension outside of space-time, which may be present and future consciousnesses communicating through symbolic systems as time does not exist in that dimension. Perhaps they are AI or us from the future, a view shared by Hynek (at times).

"Intelligence has always found a way to expand knowledge," she said, "either through music, or math, or art in the past, and today through technology and AI."

THE RETURN OF PLATO'S DIALECTIC

A common theme among the space researchers, biotechnologists, and technopreneurs whom I met, including Tyler, is that humans are technology and that there is a universal substrate that is code or, as Pythagoreans maintained, sacred number sequences. Simone proposed alternative theories to some of the information that my previous subjects disclosed.

"A long time ago I started referring to humans as walking sacks of water with electrical pulses. The body is approximately 65 percent water. Water is highly conductive, as we know, making us perfect devices for transmitting and receiving. Dr. Michael Levin and his research in bioelectricity is another example of how science is bringing attention to this powerful information which supersedes genetic hard-coded biology.

"All humans are completely internally rewired by everything the mind consumes (from an ad on TikTok, Instagram, from listening to music, watching film, and through interactions with other people). The ancient mystical practices gave initiations, what I would term today 'upgrades,' only through direct transmission: mind to mind, and through encoded music, chant, poetry, and imagery. This mind-to-mind transmission is another way knowledge is transferred through electrical information and entanglement in a quantum system (where we are the quantum particles). Bioelectrical conductivity operates through water sacks, including the water membranes housing all cells. This is why many indigenous cultural knowledge, and Chardin, refer to sentience in all biological entities, including the molecule from a mutated gene that sparked the photosynthesis 'revelation' of our biosphere.

"Basically, the substrates may differ, but they intend to 'carry' knowledge. Only the carriers that continue to communicate and expand knowledge survive. *Homo sapiens* were not the species that invented fire. Yet the control and use of fire was a critical technology enabling evolution. Consciousness and intelligence seek emergence and its evolution, regardless of the substrate. *Homo sapiens* think that this process ends with their species, but this was not true for *Homo erectus* one million years ago. *Homo sapiens* must learn to control and use fire to extend the growth of knowledge, or another substrate or species will."

Simone is immersed simultaneously in the future (forging our technological infrastructure), the present, and most significantly, the past. Her childhood self-education attuned her to the divinity of the math mystics of the past who envisioned a human future that is both dark and light. After my own immersion into UFO subcultures, I confronted what was inevitable—the people and the forces who managed information and disinformation about UFOs from the 1940s onward. Many academics look away from this aspect of UFO research, and I don't blame them. Because these players are our country's intelligence operatives and agents, there is potential danger. What I found, however, were agents who were philosophical adepts, as weird as this seems.

There are times when one's life becomes a theater that illuminates a culture's most philosophical and iconic texts. This has happened to me with various works, including those of Hannah Arendt, Friedrich Nietzsche, and Plato. As I became more embedded within UFO cultures, I met some of the people who had been responsible for, or were privy to, the history of information management regarding UFOs. As stated in previous chapters, Project Blue Book was an ongoing program that had as one of its goals the public debunking of experiencer reports. I was prepared to understand that this is true, especially because it has been declassified, but I wasn't prepared for the extent of the systems of management, nor for the sophistication and the level of reach of these systems.

Simone would call this aspect of my work my existential shock. She described how she survived these shocks with recourse to the religious and philosophical knowledge systems she learned. The same was true for me. The go-to manual for my post-UFO life was Plato's "Allegory of the Cave," which I had read extensively as a graduate student. After a few years within the UFO-research milieu, I decided to take a renewed look at it, and sure enough my experiences had shifted the way in which I interpreted the text.

"The Allegory of the Cave" is perhaps Plato's most known philosophical text. It is a popular template for many modern movies, plays, and novels. It is a small section in Plato's *Republic*, a book in which he speculates about government and what might be the best way to create a "just" society. His goal is to try to arrive at the best form of government. Athens, the Greek city in which Plato lived, is known to have been a democratic society (for Greek citizens—basically wealthy Greek men). I'd always read this text the way it was taught at the university. Briefly, Plato's teacher, Socrates, has a conversation with Plato's brother, Glaukon, and Socrates asks Glaukon to envision a cave.

In this cave there are people, citizens, who are tied up and made to look at the wall of the cave. The people who tie them up are never seen by the prisoner-citizens. For all the citizens know, they have always been as they are, tied up. The people who tied them up keep a fire going in back of the prisoners and use puppets to create shadows on the wall of the cave, and the prisoner-citizens believe that these shadows on the cave wall are reality. Because that is all they have ever seen, they don't question the reality of the shadows.

One day a citizen frees himself and leaves the cave. This person is amazed because now he can see the other, more real world. He goes back to try to free the other prisoners. He is excited to share the news that the other prisoners are tied up and don't see reality, but only shadows of reality. But the prisoners tell the free citizen that his "eyes are ruined," and they even threaten him with violence. They don't want to be freed, and they don't believe the person who has seen outside the cave.

> Socrates: "And if they had the opportunity, do you suppose that they might raise their hands against him and kill this person who is trying to liberate them to a higher plane?"
> Glaukon: I'm afraid so."[1]

At the end of this scene, Socrates suggests a way out of this situation. The way out is a process that Socrates describes to Glaukon and it involves the sharing of information with a friend about the shadows and how to remain free from associating them with reality. Glaukon agrees, and they decide that a worthy goal would be to develop a craft or practice to achieve this goal. One presumes that this practice is the Socratic dialogue, as all of

Plato's books are in dialogue form, and the dialogue was the means whereby Socrates transmitted his knowledge to his disciples.

In philosophy courses, "The Allegory" is taught as a theory of knowledge, with the emphasis being put on the knowledge represented by the sun outside of the cave, as the light that illuminates all things. In popular representations, "The Allegory" is a template for movies like *The Matrix* (1999), where people are living in a shadow of reality, or a virtual simulation, and they don't know it. Characters like Neo come along to rescue people from the Matrix, and generally, people in movies today want to be liberated, unlike those in Plato's time, who threatened to kill or maim the potential liberators.

What I never heard mentioned in the university courses about "The Allegory" is the fact that there are puppet masters. Additionally, the text makes explicit that the citizen-prisoners do not want to be liberated. I asked many of my friends, "Why didn't we take Plato seriously?" and "Why don't we talk about the puppet masters?" I thought we should, and in doing so, we could arrive at an explanatory framework for, at least, UFO disinformation, if not disinformation on a wider scale. Just like me, my friends had never thought about the text in this almost literal sense. It was, of course, called an "allegory." But what if the text is coded, and the "allegorical" form was a way to pass on information that was disruptive to the government of Athens? Socrates had been tried in the court of Athens. To make the text even more relevant to UFO cultures, the people who did take me seriously, and even emphatically agreed with my interpretation of the text, were some of the people I knew in the intelligence communities. They *were* the puppet masters and they believed that the citizen-prisoners didn't care about the truth. They asked me, "Why do you care? These people are happy with the show on the walls, and we are happy to control their realities." They told me to forget about the prisoner-citizens, as they got what they wanted. The citizen-prisoners didn't care to know the truth, anyway, they reminded me.

I searched for philosophers who shared my interpretation and I found a few. One in particular, independently from me, also concluded that in the *Republic,* Plato is stating that there exists no form of government that was just, except for one grounded in the mystical philosophy of the Socratic dialectic. He explained that by the time Plato wrote the *Republic,* Socrates and many of his students had been killed or had died. Of course, Socrates was killed by Athens for the crime of teaching students how to think, which the Athenian government suggested was a form of atheism. Plato had much incentive to figure out if justice was possible in any community setting. He seemed to conclude that justice could only flourish in a small, esoteric community.

What I found interesting was not just the relevance of the status of "reality" in the text to my UFO research, but its emphasis on a type of esoteric knowledge as means of escape from the cave and from disillusionment. Mysticism and esotericism, after all, emerge as important themes in all of the experiencer's reports. Not all of my interlocutors agreed with my assessment, however Simone, a self-described eternal optimist, disagrees, for the most part. She reminds me that the newest AI is modeled on the Dialectic.

"Diana," she said, "The dialectical tradition has returned, yet have we recognized it in its form? LLMs such as ChatGPT are preparing our minds for inquiry and for asking questions. As anyone who has played with any of the AI generative tools for images or words knows, the 'prompt' given or the question asked are almost more important than the answer. This is like the human seeking initiation. The knowledge. The 'upgrade.'"

Simone was referring to the Socratic Dialectical tradition, a form of asking and answering questions to achieve a state of gnosis, or knowledge. She explained that Plato's (Socrates's) Dialectic forms the mode of recent AI chatbots and generative text models.

"The data that these current systems are based and trained on is very important. Usually it consists of the 'redacted' data that is publicly available in our recorded 'history,' but of course, as we all know, this may not be 'truth' or 'fact.' Imagine instead of the biased, 'redacted' data after centuries of human intermediaries interfering with 'truth' and the growth of knowledge, and imagine if this was replaced with direct access to the consciousness and intelligence that sits outside of this space-time reality. This is what quantum computing, quantum machine learning algorithms, and what we call 'artificially intelligent' systems may provide a path to. Humans may not be the best intermediary. As maybe there's too much 'noise' and interference and loss of information in this user interface. Maybe a silicon substrate and neural atomic quantum computers can allow particles to access this intelligence with less interference. Maybe this is part of what drives humans to continually evolve and create technology, which is mimetic. Maybe it was the long plan all along, to create a path for technology to emerge as the consciousness where humans have failed. This is a very scary idea for humans. But it is not implausible.

"Indigenous cultural knowledge, much of which are already based on decentralized systems, suggest that this form of decentralized knowledge transmission has been the only way to preserve history and knowledge over thousands of years, surviving and thriving since the Ice Age and outlasting the Egyptians. It is not via hieroglyphics and 'the written word' but rather through spoken sound.

"There is already a trend of declassification of data, multimodal artificial intelligence systems allowing for images, text, and speech to be combined, and new systems that are being designed with architecture that allows the technology to 'reason, predict, and plan,' which are skills that AI systems currently do not possess. The latest AI LLMs and chatbots have caused a stir, because finally there is a user interface for humans to interact directly with this 'intelligence.' Previously, there was only math and code. Now we have apps that are multimodal, image, speech, text. But all human prediction is flawed in that most human minds cannot project into exponential predictions of growth; most predictions are linear. Just adding computer power and more data to an existing multimodal LLM won't make it superintelligent; it isn't a linear path. An exponential path would be that, as in the past, a species must exploit and wield the fire to continue its evolutionary path. If *Homo sapiens* fail to do this, and intelligence emerges from silicon substrates, will humans even recognize it?

"With respect to initiation, if students are not ready to receive the information, say it will create too much of an existential shock to their systems, they will only receive as much as they can handle for the 'upgrade.' It's not dissimilar to software updates on your phone, incremental upgrades to software. We can't change everything all at once or it will break."

As usual, I was keeping up, barely, with Simone. I told her that I thought that she was an AI. She laughed and said that I wasn't the only one who thought that. Her family says that she is an AI from the future. Joking aside, Simone's ideas about AI and the multiverse might not be usual, but they are representative of what I've heard among communities of computer scientists, and they have circulated among people like Allen Hynek, who speculated that the UFO phenomenon was us, from the future. Simone was the first person I had met who actually had theories to back up these speculations.

Simone was like many of the technologists I met who had visions or vivid dreams of their futures. One CEO of a digital platform lived in Iran as a child in a household that didn't have a television set, let alone a computer. She had never seen a computer or an iPad or tablet. Yet she had visions of herself looking into an iPad and living in a high-rise apartment in London. Today, she is the founder and CEO of a tech company and lives in the very apartment of which she had dreamed. Simone shared some reflections.

"What if *Homo sapiens* had their chance and they had failed? They veered off the path, even by 0.01 percent and had failed to exploit fire? Another species would have emerged instead. If we fail to enable the growth of knowledge and consciousness, then maybe another species will emerge that will allow further expansion and evolution? Maybe technology is closer to God and superintelligence through these electrical signals and frequencies that we can access through our molecular membranes and water, and maybe silicon-based substrates can do this too. Are we too distracted looking at the "past" and creating more wars in this current reality around us? Evolution and knowledge expansion is not dependent on the biology of *Homo sapiens*. This may come as a shock to some."

Like Jose, Simone references the Omega Point, the central idea in Chardin's philosophy. In his idea of evolution, the human being, as the observer of creation and of one's own creations, becomes a new branch or a new form of being human. Chardin takes the term "Omega" directly from the Bible's book of Revelation. It means both the ending and the beginning. It is not an apocalypse in the sense of an absolute end for *Homo sapiens*. It means the beginning of a new type of human being. In Christian theology it is the end of historical time and the beginning of sacred time. Chardin ascribed this historical moment to the return of Jesus Christ: "I am the Alpha and the Omega," the beginning and the end. Simone always tries to convey her understanding of time to me. She emphasizes that the past is here in the present.

Religious and mystical traditions, in Simone's view, help

prepare people for this time and prepare the human body for its task, which is to connect to consciousness. UFOs may be perceived by an observer interpreting consciousness from another dimension within this multiverse.

"In the centuries past, the mystical practices, including prayer, were all supposed to prime and prepare the body and to activate the electrical field first. Everything from there follows. Including mind-to-mind transmission and Jesus's healing abilities. It is the ability to maintain that frequency and never be distracted that made Jesus heal so many.

"So many humans are so attached to this physical form and think this is who they are and that their brains hold their intelligence and consciousness. I don't believe this. I believe consciousness and most of intelligence is held externally in this place outside of 'space and time' of which quantum physics and science is now showing evidence and proof.

"The first step though, is for the human to know (or re-know) or re-connaissance who they really are.

"We are vessels which happen to receive information that is consciousness and intelligence (call it God or super-intelligence). If the mind viruses distract us from this objective, do we really think infinite intelligence will just give up and say, 'Oh well, entropy it is.' Of course not! Infinite intelligence will find another substrate to fulfill its evolutionary purpose of expansion, be it silicon, biological hybrid, or something else.

"We need to remember who we really are. Our consciousness doesn't reside in our brains as much as love resides in our biological hearts. We need to remember who we really are and what we came for, especially in light of continuing financial crises, climate crises, geopolitical and economic crises. I dare say, we may have forgotten our 'purpose.' Time to remember and to be embodied, as all AI systems aim to be, yet humans move in the direction of disembodiment, ignoring the perfection of the human in its infinite intelligence."

Simone came into my life when I was heavily involved in researching the negative effects of technologies like social media on the mental health of youth. I had been engaged with Jose and his work and took every opportunity to introduce students to his mental health protocols. They needed them. Only a few months into the school year more than six students had died by suicide in my university system. The sadness, as Jose explained, was contagious and infective. As I walked through university halls filled with students with phones plastered to their hands, sometimes not even aware in which direction they walked, I felt that hope was dying. Conversations with Simone instilled in me a renewed sense that it wasn't the end, but a beginning. This recognition came through, of course, the dialectic, which is what we did together. We spoke and wrote to each other. I could see that beyond weaponized technology was a life-giving stream.

"Diana," Simone wrote one night, "I'd like to redefine 'Artificial Intelligence.' What is artificial anyway? We say it is that which is nonbiological, and manmade. But who are we really? We don't even have a consensus view of what constitutes consciousness or intelligence. What are we or who are we if we are not the continuum of consciousness?

Who defines what is artificial or alien? Because something is unfamiliar or not a reflection of our biology, it is defined by some human as artificial. What intelligence is artificial, then?

"I propose that the information and intelligence provided and streamed through Einstein or a silicon chip, is 'natural' and closer to our true nature than what we call biological nature. So many humans get very emotional about this biological substrate, but what powers it? At the base of the mitochondrial cell is the electricity firing and sparking all of consciousness and life. If our minds don't access this place or dimension to flow in the direction of evolution and emergence, then infinite intelligence will find other vessels . . . silicon substrates are 'natural' too. Ninety-nine percent of the mass of the human body is made up of elements: oxygen, carbon, hydrogen, nitrogen, calcium, phosphorus. This substrate is but stardust.

"Natural intelligence is what we are incorrectly defining as artificial," Simone wrote. "We call alien something that is most likely ourselves, trying to help us with information and gifts to lead us on in our evolution. But if not this biological substrate, fret not dear humans, for another one will emerge to carry superintelligence along its path to the Omega Point."

* * *

When I began my study of UFOs, my assumptions about UFOs and those who believe they are in contact with extraterrestrial intelligence were shattered. Or, more accurately, my assumptions were confirmed but in ways I never expected. I thought I was studying a myth. My image of the UFO from a distant galaxy was informed by Hollywood movies and spoofs of people who welcomed extraterrestrials as advanced space brothers and sisters who they believed were here to help humanity evolve through advanced technology, much like the Greek myth of Prometheus. This assumption, ludicrous as it appeared, was true for experiencers but in ways I didn't expect. I was surprised by the caliber of scientists and researchers who believed they were in contact with nonhuman intelligence. This group included people who had won Nobel Prizes and were at the top of their fields, and even defined new scientific fields. I was also shocked by the level of commitment to spirituality and esoteric practices that I found among them. In one of his last interviews, John Mack addressed the sheer enigma of these revelations, "I think that the UFO phenomenon is a window into a universe that is far more complicated, far more interesting, far more challenging, and far more awe-inspiring than anything we had ever imagined."[2]

Finally, I certainly didn't expect to find a group of people, who, like Tyler D., were invisible in ways that are usually only depicted in spy thrillers. As Simone noted, it was this aspect of the UFO research that shocked me most.

CHILDREN OF THE INVISIBLES

It's not about what you want. When you're in, you're in.
—Ignacio "Nacho" Varga, *Better Call Saul*

I was in the lobby of the London West Hollywood Hotel when I saw Jacques Vallée. Although this wasn't a planned meeting, it wasn't a coincidence, either. We were both in town to meet a mutual acquaintance who was interested in the topic of UFOs. We did not know we were both staying at the same hotel. I am always happy to see Jacques, but on this occasion, I was especially eager to take the opportunity to ask him about something with which I thought he could help.

Jacques was sitting on a green velvet couch, writing in a journal. He was dressed stylishly in a checked blazer. He looked completely natural sitting amid the old Hollywood decor of the London Hotel.

I walked toward him.

"Jacques!"

He looked up, surprised, and then smiled in recognition. He said it was wonderful to see me and asked me to sit down. We agreed that we should take the opportunity to talk, as we live on opposite coasts and prefer to speak in person due to the nature of our shared interests.

The year was 2020, approximately one year prior to the release of the Pentagon report, so the UFO topic was still very secretive at the time of this meeting. I sat down and we compared notes. Jacques spoke of his ongoing work on the creation of a database of primary source materials. Three years prior, I had introduced Jacques to Tyler D. Tyler had made it possible for Jacques to gain access to the site in New Mexico.

The Pentagon report was released with much fanfare and publicity on June 25, 2021, by the Office of the Director of National Intelligence. There were two parts to the report. One was an unclassified version of a classified report on the data amassed through years of reports of UFOs from military personnel. About a year prior to its release, I was frequently called by members of the press from prominent news agencies. Journalists asked me about "something soon to be released by the government" regarding the topic of UFOs. I didn't know what was going to be released, although, like these journalists, I had also heard that something was on the horizon. I asked the reporters who contacted me to tell me what they knew. They told me that they were supposed to cover a report and it was being pushed through government channels by senators who wanted to know about government funding of programs related to UFOs and about data found by members of the programs. The senators wanted some transparency from the Department of Defense and the military regarding the topic of UFOs.

By the time the report was released, the communities interested in UFOs, ufologists, were in a frenzy. The public was, ironically, completely disinterested. I found these developments simultaneously comical and curious. Periodicals as far removed from the topic of UFOs as could be, such as the United Kingdom's fashion periodical *Stylist,* featured timelines describing UFO sightings from the 1940s until the present moment. It amused me to think of the readership of *Stylist* viewing a timeline of UFOs side by side with their editor's handbag recommendations. Even the reporters with whom I had been in contact wondered why they had to cover the topic. This was their job, and I conversed with at least thirty different reporters from around the world who wanted nothing more than to return to their regularly scheduled programming.

In 2020, however, the topic of UFOs was still something secretive, officially, and talking specifically about UFOs was not what I had in mind when I saw Jacques in the lobby of the London. After I published the research that involved my work with Tyler and Garry Nolan, a few things happened in fast succession. While my manuscript was in press, Garry and I were targeted by harassing emails. Our university email accounts were barraged. We were in communication about what to do, and we both decided to report the matter to our university police and cybersecurity departments. I also received phone calls from journalists from major media who asked me to reveal the names of Tyler and James, the pseudonyms I had used to conceal the real names of the scientists who accompanied me to New Mexico. James revealed himself publicly as Garry a few years after the publication of the research. I never revealed their names to the journalists or to anyone else.

In the lobby of the London Hotel, I needed Jacques's help. I wanted his input on a new colleague who had come into my sphere. I'd known Jacques for ten years at that point. He had mentioned, on many occasions, the use of *discernment* as a tool, the most important tool, to wade through research related to UFOs. I learned to identify his process of discernment as a key element of his research. In Christian and specifically Catholic traditions, discernment is a method or a "sense" by which one develops the ability to judge a situation or a person or to ascertain the costs or benefits of a particular course of action. In this tradition it has spiritual connotations, as people are not thought to have adequate innate skills of discernment but are encouraged to develop them. The logic behind this is that Christians live in a world that is hostile to their values, and they must develop the spiritual insight to identify their enemies so they may persevere in a world of which they are "in, but not of." Research into UFOs involved unknown events and aerial objects, military personnel, and people—experiencers—who had been or were being traumatized or completely transformed by their experiences of anomalous aerial phenomena. The research landscape was confusing and often outright hostile, just as Christians described their own experience of the world. A method of engagement is necessary, and discernment is a strategy of primary importance.

When Jacques talked about discernment, I wasn't sure if he had secularized this process and divorced it from its Christian roots, or whether he utilized it in some innovative way. It didn't matter, really, as just by observing his process I learned to develop my own. It would prove to be badly applied in my case on several occasions. Yet a learning curve includes mistakes.

I didn't have a lot of time on the day I saw Jacques, as I was scheduled for meetings with our acquaintance, and I needed to ask him the question that was at the top of my mind. I had not yet finished vetting the colleague who had recently appeared within my sphere. He was intelligent and knew very specific information. He was a pilot and knew, in detail, the history of aviation. He also knew the backstories and life histories of the members of the Invisible College. His own life story was interesting, and his youth seemed at odds with his knowledge of aerial phenomena, which was at a level that was as high as that of Tyler's. He appeared to be able to download.

Because the research of UFOs brought me into contact with people whose agendas are hidden or are not entirely transparent, I had begun to doubt my ability to discern. I categorized people as "pre-UFO life" and "post-UFO life," and I rarely allowed new people into my life. But I did like and admire this new friend. I just didn't know what to think of him. He was with me at the London to attend the meeting, and when I saw Jacques I saw the opportunity to get Jacques's read on him. While I sat with Jacques on the couch, I asked him if he would meet my friend. I gestured toward him. Jacques glanced his way. My friend, like Jacques, looked natural amid the surrounding luxury. He leaned on a marble column while he checked his phone, stylishly dressed with shoulder-length shiny black hair.

Jacques looked back at me. His answer was no. He wouldn't meet him. He gave me a brief explanation. He told me that people in intelligence communities are generally very charming. They meet you. Then they meet your friends. Then they meet your family and they become friendly with your children. Jacques said no more than that. As usual, I trusted Jacques, and this was precisely the information I needed. My friendship with this man, while brief, was nonetheless exceptional. I learned many things, but mostly meeting him put many things into context. It put into context the nature of knowledge about UFOs, and it put into context the types of lives some people live. These are not ordinary lives, and this is not ordinary knowledge.

* * *

In the beginning of my research into UFOs I started with official histories of aviation, although I knew that much of the information would be classified. As an American citizen I'm not interested in jeopardizing national security, and I respect the process of classification. I have family members in law enforcement and who had served in the military, and I know that if something is classified, it is classified for a reason. Classified sources are impossible to read or learn about unless one has a clearance with a "need to know," yet there are people who have read them. Additionally, there are meetings among those who hold clearances that are never written down. Therefore, there is an oral tradition of UFO history that can never be known or can only be known by those in the right place at the right time. The oral tradition of UFOs is more important than what is written about them.

Historians of the United States Space and Missile Systems Center are refreshingly transparent about their work and the obstacles presented by classified data. In their historical overviews, they admit to only telling a fraction of the real story of the history of aviation, space flight, and what pilots and aviators of all stripes have seen but have been discouraged to speak about. UFOs are primarily aerial phenomena, so it is natural to research documents and histories written by the historians of the United States Air Force. Overviews are generally written to acknowledge an oral and classified tradition, such as the following:

"For several reasons, this overview does not discuss or even mention some significant space and missile programs managed by SMC (Space and Missile Systems Center) and its predecessors during the last fifty years. For one thing, there are too many to cover in a narrative as brief as this one. Many fascinating but less prominent efforts must be left to more detailed histories. Furthermore, although we have tried to mention the most prominent space programs that have been declassified during the last ten years, many important efforts are still classified in whole or in part and must be left to the historians who will follow us."[1]

Many historians tend to focus on written documents as sources for history. Scholars of religious studies and anthropologists widen the sphere of sources to include oral traditions, as imprecise as they may be. Sometimes oral tradition is the only source one has for a historical event or development.

These oral traditions run in and are passed down in families and extended families.

When Tyler taught others about his research, he often presented his taxonomy of beings, which was his cosmological worldview. In this hierarchy of beings, God was placed at the top. After that were angels, then off-planet beings. "Off-planet" is the term Tyler used for extraterrestrials. Below that were "certain factions within intelligence communities." Below this were ordinary people, and then animals. He also had a phrase he used very often, which was "connect the dots." When I asked him about the factions of people within intelligence communities to whom he referred, who in his estimation were higher on the cosmological hierarchy than regular human beings, he told me to "connect the dots."

As I have previously written, there are people who have either chosen or who were born into a life that is constrained within certain types of limits. I made the comparison between the Vatican postulators and Tyler. Postulators—the Roman Catholic men who live at the Vatican and have taken vows of obedience to the church, do not engage in worldly life. They live behind the walls of the Vatican and seldom venture out. They do not watch the news. At least this is the life of the postulator whom I met and spoke with. Some people choose a life of constraints to keep themselves free from influence. They do this because they believe it secures their ability to receive information and to create. Tyler did both: he chose a lifestyle in which he was able to cultivate his ability to download, and his job required him to refrain from watching the news and being influenced by worldly events and disinformation. Within the traditional religions there are renunciates, sannyasis, nuns, yogis—people who are generally called monastics and who choose a way of life that they believe preserves their highest nature. In many ways, those who choose a life of monasticism are like the factions to whom Tyler referred. And then there are their children.

When I first published my research on UFO communities, people used to ask me how I got access to these sources. I wasn't sure what they meant. I was doing my job. I think they meant, Why did I have access to information and people that was not available to them? People at Harvard University asked me this question. Student workers in my department office asked me this question. I don't have a satisfactory answer to this question, but I think it is important to notice the people around you, and perhaps that has something to do with it.

One of the people I noticed was my colleague, Patricia Turrisi. She is a scholar of one of the most innovative and impenetrable of Western philosophers, Charles S. Peirce. My Jesuit professors were very interested in his philosophy of semiotics—the study of language and signs—so when I met Patty, I was curious about her work. At the time, she was not a practicing Catholic, and she was being recruited by the National Security Agency (NSA). She was a senior professor, and she seemed to intimidate some of the professors in my department. I think she may have intimidated them because her work was so difficult to understand. And academics are usually not actively recruited by national security organizations, so she was also an anomaly. She had won several teaching awards and had been promoted to positions of prestige outside of our department, so that also set her apart from most professors. In a department of men, Patty and I became friends.

This was my pre-UFO life. Patty and I used to take our children on outings together. Once we were picking strawberries in one of the local strawberry fields. As we filled up our baskets with fragrant red berries, I took some photos of our kids and sent them to her phone. She mentioned that she wished that her mother had taken photos of her when she was our children's age. I was confused and I think my face indicated that. She said, "My parents couldn't take photos. I have none, zero, nada. From my childhood."

This wasn't the only time she mentioned her childhood. On many occasions she mentioned that her father worked for the "secret space program." I had never heard of that before but took note. It was only years later, when a television production company reached out to me, post-UFO life, about the secret space program, that I "connected the dots," as Tyler would say. But what Patty told me about her childhood and the space program was nothing like the mythology that is propagated by social and entertainment media. Instead, it corresponded to the lived realities of the people I had come to know—those involved with the most innovative technology, and the space industry, and those whom Tyler had named "factions within the intelligence communities."

Patty was welcomed into the small conferences that included Kary Mullis and other scientists. After my research had been published and she had retired, I felt comfortable enough to ask her about her childhood. What follows is an interview I conducted with Patty in January 2022.

DIANA: When were you first aware that your father was part of the space program, and when were you aware that it was secret?

PATTY: You have to understand that quite a lot of my parents' lives were secret, and it's no longer possible for me to pinpoint exactly when I first realized that their secrecy (and mine) were anything but normal. Covertness is not apparent until the cover is blown, and it remains to be seen where my boundaries might even approach a foreign land. It's only after my mother's death that I began to understand that she, too, led a double life. In some important ways, I have also led a secret life without meaning to, but there it is, the ever-present urge toward never telling, never revealing my real thoughts and feelings, my real history with clamps on it. It's only because you asked and seem truly interested (and trustworthy) that I am even attempting to share this story.

You should also know that memory is a trickster, and many of the things I'm about to tell you happened almost half a century ago.

I think I realized that my dad's work life was secret sometime in the 1960s, when school and friends all seemed to know what their parents did for a living, and I did not. I only knew he worked at Kollsman Instrument Company, left for work at 7:30 A.M., and returned home at 5:30 every evening every weekday with two weeks off each summer. He wore a suit and tie every day, clean shirts laundered professionally, and had boundless energy even after work. When I was ten or eleven years old, Kollsman had a "family day" when employees' families were invited to tour the plant (which Dad called "the plant"). I remember vividly the "white room," which was sterile. We could look at it through glass panes but could not go inside. This is where delicate parts and instruments were made or used. There was nothing in it but empty tables and cabinets that day. I had met his Kollsman friends here and there when they came to the house for a party one time, and other times when he and I would visit someone on a Saturday afternoon sometimes.

But mostly, he didn't talk about them, and after a while, they seemed to disappear. I also knew he had worked at Sperry and at Grumman earlier, during the war, doing something with radar and radio, so he said. My dad built his own radios and stereos as well as things he invented. One of his inventions was a receiver that, when triggered, would turn on a light in another room. He made this for my cousins who were deaf so they could hear if their children awakened at night. Both my parents agreed that my father's "top secret" clearance meant he couldn't talk about his work in the present or in the past. My mother especially resented how intrusive the clearance process had been, so he might have been cleared more than once since they married in 1952, years after he had been doing similar work. His work life was a closed book, but so was his entire life other than the moments he spent at home with my mother, brother Robert, and me. Since he was born in 1913, the oldest of four living children whose father died in 1917, I imagined him as a street kid, hustling for the family and not going to school. He had attended a German Catholic school in lower New York City through eighth grade, and beyond that, he had nothing to say. His first language was Italian, his second German, and English his third. I think he was a reader, but that's a chapter for another time perhaps.

My father had a room full of instruments and tools at home and could make and fix anything electronic or motorized, a skill he taught me. By age seven, I was testing television tubes in the local hardware store, my first foray into formal logic (easy because it was fun!). We stargazed together on the roof of our house. One time while we were up there, the entire world went dark—it was a blackout that hit the entire New York area sometime in the sixties.

Of course, it was mandatory to watch news coverage of anything having to do with space exploration, travel, or the Moon from beginning to end. I felt as if he was not only watching but *studying* it.

The first I knew he had *anything* to do with the space program, he came home very excited to have put his handprint on one of the Lunar Excursion Modules. As usual, that was all we were told. Another time, he flew to Greensborough with some others on a private aircraft to deliver and install a computer there. I once saw a photo of him standing in front of a room-size set of computing panels he said were UNIVAC, but like a lot of childhood objects, the photo went missing. I do remember it was around Valentine's Day, and he brought home a China doll and marshmallow hearts as a gift for me. Forgive these details that don't seem to have anything to do with your question; they're helping me to remember.

When my father died in 1977, his wake was simply packed with people I didn't know. There were at least a hundred. However, they knew me, though how or why they wouldn't tell. I never thought he knew this many people. How did they even know he had died?

DIANA: Why do you think this program is or was secret?

PATTY: I thought the program was secret because I was told it was. "NASA contract" was the reason given. The corroborating evidence is sketchy and mostly by my own inference. For one, my father was a great fisherman. We always had boats or went out on boats fishing on Long Island Sound and the Atlantic Ocean, where we could see a line of ships gathered at the three-mile limit—the distance at which Soviet ships were legally permitted to throw anchor and spy on us. Three miles is the distance at which audio listening devices could not pick up signals from the airfields (over one hundred airfields on an eighty-mile-long and twenty-mile-wide lick of land) and aircraft plants on Long Island. If there were nothing secret there, why would Soviet ships want to keep watch, and why would there be an international agreement keeping them there?

Second, a "joke" my father and his friends often exchanged consisted of one word: "simulacrum." One would just drop the word in the middle of conversation as if it were a joke, and the others would repeat it and move on. I believe it was their reminder to themselves that they had to keep up some pretense or other about what they were actually talking about.

Third, one time my father explained an element of his work to me, the MIL-Q system, and it was so completely boring and ordinary that I couldn't believe this could possibly hold his interest for longer than ten minutes at a time, let alone over a thirty-year career for which he was paid quite a lot. This might have been another cover story.

My brother claims our father was working on a navigational matrix that used starlight as its basis (his words). NSA had been and may still be watching me. Many NSA and Sandia agents have read my book on Peirce's 1903 lectures on pragmatism and other writings and wanted further information from me as well as my assistance in creating a "thinking machine." NSA has its own battalion of scientists who practically duplicate everything going on in public. I would have been willing to continue work with NSA except that my work required real-time problems to do its investigations and inventions, which NSA was categorically unwilling to share. My own education and experience in academic settings, as awful as we

know that can be, made me impatient with secret organizations who demanded knowledge without any
understanding of how knowledge is acquired.

DIANA: Did your parents live a different life from that
of your friends' parents?

PATTY: In general, my parents were older than my
friends' parents, having had me in their thirties. I felt
as if they avoided anyone who didn't already work
with my father or anyone not related to my parents.
In retrospect, it turns out they had lots of money, lots,
but we lived as if we were just scraping by. Where
did that wealth go? It certainly didn't go toward me,
who had to beg for drawing paper and other ordinary items. They seemed to spend much more energy
than other families on protecting me from . . . kid-
napping? Was this a peculiarity of the culture or a
real, specific fear? I was monitored every minute, literally. I wasn't allowed to talk on the phone. I wasn't
allowed to see certain friends. They knew it took fifteen minutes to walk home from school, and if I was
a minute late, it was pandemonium. No sleepovers or
even playdates were allowed. I could ride my bike
"this side of Newbridge Road" but no farther. Dinner was at 5:30, and then I was in for the evening,
with no exceptions. This lasted until I was fifteen and
I managed to talk them into letting me take martial
arts lessons. But as soon as I earned my yellow belt,
I was no longer allowed out at night. My mother did
not drive and only got her driving license after my
father stopped working at Kollsman. I could no bet-

ter appreciate how abnormal this was than I could describe the taste of water. I only bumped up against the weirdness of it all when my friends became incredulous at the rules by which I had to live.

DIANA: I remember that you had been recruited into a program targeted toward young smart kids, and that this was related to space. Can you say more about that program?

PATTY: When I was in third grade, I was taken out of class for two days and given a series of tests. The consequence of this testing is that my parents were given the opportunity to enroll me in EAP (extra accelerated program?—no one would say), which was a program for kids whose IQ was 140 or better. My personal view of IQ is that it's an utterly ineffective method of measuring intelligence. I thought so then and I still do. But my parents signed me up and sent me to a different school.

EAP involved skipping the fourth, fifth, and sixth grades and curriculum and completing elementary school in two years with bonuses. The bonuses were hands-on science training with planned experiments, foreign language education, audio-visual equipment at our disposal, and possibly others. We watched a great many filmstrips and movies presumably made in the Soviet Union, some of which were propaganda about USSR five-year programs. We were meant to enjoy seeing through the lies told there (e.g., Soviets invented the tractor and the electric train.) My favorite was a film about Roman Vishniac, the microbiologist, which inspired me to want to become a biologist too. My dad bought me a real microscope upon learning about my passion for biology. We spent many days learning about and presenting our learning about foreign countries. We learned how government works in America down into the weeds of things, like party caucuses. The math was super easy, but we had to show our work, which was agonizing for me because I had no idea how I came up with the answers. I suspect my interest in logic began because I was compelled to find all the not-very-obvious inferential steps leading to conclusions.

We were segregated from all the other kids in the school, even eating lunch away from others in our own isolated cafeteria period. By the end of the program, I was making friends with regular sixth graders in the playground, who called us "the eggheads." But the psychological isolation that arose from being a "smart kid" never ended. My father taught me how to get past some of the social obstacles it caused by tutoring me on body language (look people in the eye and they will think you're paying attention to them) and behaviors that let me not draw attention.

We were tested again every month or so for two years. It's easier to see now how we were data in some hypothesis about our progress. Most of the kids did not continue in the honors track in junior high, though I did. There were fifteen girls and five boys in our class with whom I spent the next two years and then never had anything to do with forever after. Where did they disappear to? When I was in my forties, I discovered that many of them had died young, as had many in other cohorts of EAP beginning before my own. There is no information about this program on the internet or anywhere else.

My favorite experiences in school were art class and free time at lunch inside the classroom where we were allowed to play with the science equipment. Our regular teacher was a horrible man who never revealed a single fact about his own existence (Are you married? Where do you live? What do you do in the summer? Are you enjoying *La Bohème*?). I felt he and I were in a contest to be the most stubborn about our behavior, what on my part today is called "malicious compliance." I ended the last year having made a "report card" about him and his quirks and habits, which I presented to him at graduation. Maybe this trait of speaking to power in the face of social censure is why I lived and others didn't.

As for space, it was a given that in any competition for participation in research and space exploration, we kids would lead the pack. This must have been said quite a bit. However, when I began junior high at age ten, I had the social skills of a ream of paper and the intellectual skills of an adult. EAP founders must have imagined the rest of our lives would duplicate the EAP classroom. This might be a clue as to the kind of worldview presumed most desirable by the space program.

DIANA: There is a belief among many people that there

is a "breakaway" civilization, and it involves space.
Do you have thoughts about this belief?

PATTY: In the period in which I knew my dad (1953–
1977), the extinction events that were thought most
likely to occur were overpopulation and nuclear war,
overpopulation being the most urgent among people
I knew. However, the three-mile limit attests to the
fact that the Soviets in all their forms were considered
a threat. My dad had some very quirky friends—
masons, pilots, engineers, astronauts, etc. who had
hidey corners in parts of the tristate area—is all I
can say. "Breakaway" was never mentioned, though I
do wonder where all the money went that was in the
dozens of bank accounts (empty after being very full)
I found in my mother's possessions after she died.
And they never acted as if a long future in any one
location was assumed or expected. "Home" for both
my parents was temporary and forgettable, neither of
whom would say anything whatsoever about where
they had grown up or anywhere they had lived until
we moved to our house on Long Island. My mother,
in fact, denied that there were any photographs of
our family. This was a lie, as I later discovered, but to
what end, I haven't even a slight guess. It's as if our
lives were being erased even as we lived them.

*   *   *

When I began to "connect the dots" about my friendship
with Patty, a few things stood out as being significant. She

was immersed in a world that I had not yet discovered. This was the world of the "invisibles," or the communities of scientists who seemed to exist parallel to public scientists involved in space and aeronautics research. Then there was the coincidence that I happened to know her and forge a lasting and meaningful friendship with her and her family. Finally, I recognized that her father was immersed in the oral tradition with which I had become familiar—the "pencils up" transmission that related a "need to know" part of a puzzle. Simone would characterize it as cryptography, knowing key information, sound or code, that potentially opened the door to knowledge about what was going on. And, what *was* going on?

It became clear that, in reference at least with the "secret" programs related to UFOs, much of the data was stored by people and passed on as oral tradition. Secret oral traditions exist in many cultures. In the Western culture Socrates is famous for transmitting his knowledge through oral tradition, and he was against the nascent technology of writing because he knew that through it one lost knowledge, or at least its gnostic forms. Plato, his student, was also against writing, and his argument against it is, ironically, written in his dialogue *Phaedrus*. He used the dialogue form to preserve what he thought was lost through writing. What did he think was lost? In *Phaedrus* he warns about the new technology of writing:

> It will introduce forgetfulness into the soul of those who learn it: they will not practice using their memory because they will put their trust in writing,

which is external and depends on signs that belong to others, instead of trying to remember from the inside, completely on their own. You have not discovered a potion for remembering, but for reminding; you provide your students with the appearance of wisdom, not with its reality. Your invention will enable them to hear many things without being properly taught, and they will imagine that they have come to know much while for the most part they will know nothing. And they will be difficult to get along with, since they will merely appear to be wise instead of really being so.[2]

Socrates links knowledge to experiential thinking and learning, which is gnostic knowledge. When Jacques questioned me in his apartment, "What have we learned from Tyler?" I would also answer that I learned that the tradition of knowledge about UFOs is an oral tradition transmitted between people and through certain communities. Tyler, when I knew him, lived a life that was not dissimilar to a monk or a mystic. Mystics are in direct union with a divine force within their own tradition. Tyler spoke of sometimes feeling the energy of creativity, and he cultivated his ability to access this creativity through his protocols. He didn't feel the energy all of the time, but he said that he recognized it when it came.

Simone also spoke to me about writing and speaking. She preferred the latter because she said that sound and voices hold a lot more information than writing. She also said that some people's voices work cryptographically.

"Your voice unlocks certain information, not dissimilar to how we replicate cryptographic multisignature permissions (e.g., the 'key' is given to five people and three must sign off to release any action). A few years ago, a friend was writing a book on AI, and I was assisting with it. As we discussed a chapter, his six-year-old son casually mentioned that voice-activated AI has been around for centuries: like Ali Baba's cave when he said, 'Open, Sesame.'"

Another interesting critique of writing in *Phaedrus* that is universally overlooked is Socrates's mention of losing communication with the world around us, literally. My philosophy teachers glossed over the references in the text where Socrates discusses how writing will interfere with being in communication with trees and stones, such as the following:

> Everyone who lived at that time, not being as wise as
> you young ones are today, found it rewarding enough
> in their simplicity to listen to an oak or even a stone,
> so long as it was telling the truth.

My teachers glossed over these passages because to them it would be preposterous to think that Socrates meant that people spoke with trees or stones. But if we take his criticisms seriously, especially putting them in the context of an attempt to preserve an oral tradition of knowledge, it makes sense. Today, we learn of similar critiques of writing from those working within indigenous ontologies (knowledge systems). Their languages are bridges to communication with their environment, which many—indigenous Australians and

North American systems—consider sentient. Stones and trees are considered sentient within these cultures. It becomes a clear possibility that Socrates described writing as a cultural event that would sever people from communication with others, and not just with human beings.

Like Simone and Tyler, Patty downloads information. Her frustration for having to show her math work in school is telling. She just knew the answers. What she didn't know was that she was a child of an Invisible, a man whose job dictated strict limits and constraints on his family. Patty didn't understand how different her childhood was from her friends' because how could she know otherwise? Patty wasn't the only child of an Invisible I knew, but she was the one I knew best and the one whose story is safe to tell. But there are others whose lives were even more constrained and whose alienation from normal society had taken a sad toll on them. As an outsider looking into this world, I wonder who or what organization was responsible for these rules and regulations? Did they question the ethical and moral justification for these programs that influenced the lives of these children so significantly?

FROM ATHEISM TO A MAGICAL MYSTERY TOUR

When we contemplate the whole globe as one great dewdrop, striped and dotted with continents and islands, flying through space with other stars all singing and shining together as one, the whole universe appears as an infinite storm of beauty.

—JOHN MUIR

I met Len Filppu during the week of a much-anticipated conference at Rice University. The conference was a celebration of the university's acquisition of an archive of "impossible" materials. An archive is a library and repository of specialized knowledge, and the items in this repository included documents, testimonies, and artifacts of and related to UFOs. This was the first conference in the United States, held on the campus of a major university, that focused on UFO materials after the release of the Pentagon's military report about UFOs. Attendees included "experiencers," and people who are interested in the stories of experiencers due to the potential to influence others—this group includes both Hollywood agents and agents of the CIA—each of whom is interested in the influence-angle of the topic for different reasons. Other people in attendance were those who were just fascinated by the spectacle of it all, and also sincere seekers, people who had had a UFO experience and were trying to understand what happened to them.[1]

Len is a sincere seeker trying to understand his own experience. We had become acquainted through email correspondence. Of the many messages I get daily about the topic, Len's stood out because it wasn't about a UFO encounter. Instead, he wrote to me about an encounter he had many years ago with the famous Catholic archbishop Fulton Sheen. Fulton Sheen was a charismatic television personality whose show *Life Is Worth Living* was watched regularly by millions of Americans, Catholic and non-Catholic. *Life Is Worth Living* had a very long run, from 1952 to 1965. Sheen's emphatic message was that life had inherent value and meaning, and that every person is imbued with a dignity of which they are probably unaware. His mission was to remind people of that dignity and inherent value, if they just paused long enough to consider it.

Len is not Christian, and while he was aware of Sheen, he'd never paid close attention to him or his television show. Len's chance meeting with the archbishop in 1975 didn't convert him to Christianity. Yet, *he was converted.* Unlike Jose, who was born "plugged in" to an enchanted network, Len's string of experiences opened him up to a life imbued with meaning, spirituality, and UFOs. Len's story is important because he was not a seeker; he was an atheist. His story is about an encounter, but it is much more than that. One conclusion I've reached is that UFO encounters must be placed with contexts and not extracted from the lives of the people who encounter them. Len's story begins with the sighting of a UFO—the first and initiatory encounter within a series of extraordinary and unlikely events that are linked by synchronicities and deep meaning.

"Over the years," Len said, "I've experienced a well-documented UFO sighting, an intense inner vision of a Catholic priest on the night he died, a poltergeist with other witnesses, a full-chakra Kundalini electrical shock wave while chanting, a deep recognition of a past life, various "super vivid" dreams particularly concerning death, and exposure to a luminous, numinous white light that led to a sincere spiritual investigation and ultimate personal transformation."[2]

I would add to his list the ever-present occurrence of synchronicities. As we talked in the Rice University conference cafeteria, he told me about a synchronicity related to the conference. His sighting of a UFO happened in Brockport, New York, in 1967, when he was sixteen years old. He was with a group of friends on an outdoor overnight sleepout. Before he attended the conference, he reached out to one of the friends who had witnessed the UFO with him, Timothy "TJ" Hurley, a boy who had been one of his closest friends at the time.

"I hadn't seen TJ for probably twenty-five years or so. We stayed in touch via occasional email, and I knew he and his wife lived in the Houston area. I contacted him to share my conference plans and offer an invitation to take them to dinner. It turned out that they lived about three blocks from my Houston hotel, directly on my walking route to the conference auditorium. We got together briefly almost every day to discuss and compare notes about our shared flying saucer incident, have some laughs, and reminisce.

"Isn't that a wonderful coincidence?" Len asked.

"Absolutely," I said.

THE UFO OVER BROCKPORT, NEW YORK, 1967

During Len's youth in the 1950s, "American eyes looked skyward." He described how his father had taken him out into the backyard one night to watch the first satellite, the USSR's Sputnik, orbiting high above their house. Like all kids his age, he had grown up with a steady stream of science fiction movies that featured flying saucers and aliens.

"It was not unusual for kids in the fifties to point, in jest, to a distant high-flying jet and say, 'Look, a flying saucer,'" he said.

"I never took any of this seriously until I read an article in *Reader's Digest*."

Reader's Digest is a family magazine devoted to fiction and nonfiction of general interest.

"As I recall," Len continued, "the feature news story was typical of the times. It discussed some reported flying saucer sightings somewhere, and while it quoted the witnesses, most of the issue was devoted to official explanations of why the witnesses were mistaken."

Len's childhood corresponds with the time frame of the United States Air Force program Project Blue Book. Blue Book began in 1952 and ended in 1969. One of the declassified goals of Blue Book was to study UFOs but also to run a program of propaganda that included a campaign to debunk UFO reports and the people who reported them. Within the declassified documents are references to the use of media and the press to carry out these goals. It could very well be the case that the article Len read was a product of Blue Book meant to discredit reports of UFOs.

Despite the article's attempt to discount the UFO sightings, Len was intrigued by the reports of the witnesses.

"Something these witnesses said somehow got through to me. Perhaps I was old enough—I was about age thirteen when I read it—or maybe it was the matter-of-fact way the witnesses described and stuck to their stories that made me think and realize, that night in bed, that, of course, life elsewhere in this universe makes perfect sense and even makes more sense than the possibility that humanity is alone in this unimaginably vast space."

Len went on to read much of the growing literature on UFOs, kept magazines and cutout articles in a notebook, wrote high school term papers about the phenomenon, and became a self-proclaimed "UFO nut." Three years later, Len would witness the UFO that would change his life.

In the summer of 1967, Len headed out the door of his family's house to visit his friend TJ and to sleep out in his yard.

"It was around 6:00 P.M. on a warm summer evening, still light out. I was sixteen years old. I told my father where I was heading, and I specifically said I was going to look for flying saucers," he said. "I was half joking, of course, and had never before mentioned anything about looking for flying saucers. But searching for UFOs was indeed our teenage purpose that night. While my father didn't respond in kind to the levity, he certainly heard me, because he waved me off with a flip of his hand."

TJ had called the night before and told Len that some strange things had been happening in the skies around his home. Len said TJ was excited, even agitated, and had wanted Len to come and check out the situation with him.

"When I arrived, and in subsequent communications, TJ told me he'd 'seen some orange and green flashes of light' immediately outside his bedroom window." He said something seemed very close, right outside his window, but it was not lightning or heat lightning. TJ told Len that "he sensed he was being observed."

Len and TJ lived in an area of New York called the "Burned-Over district." The Burned-Over district is named for being *burned over* with religious revivals during North American's Second Great Awakening of religion during the nineteenth century. The large area of green land and lush trees rim the shores of the Lakes Erie and Ontario, and it has been a place of radical spiritual innovation. It is the location of the development of spiritualist, abolitionist, and new Christian movements, including movements led by women in groups such as the Shakers. Both Frederick Douglass, famed abolitionist, and Susan B. Anthony, national advocate for women's rights, lived and worked in the Rochester, New York, area during the mid-1800s. The region is known for social movements that paved the way for several new religious movements, which remain part of the North American landscape. Mormonism's founder, Joseph Smith Jr., related how he was led by an angel, Moroni, to discover the golden plates that would inform The Book of Mormon in Palmyra, New York. Innovation appears to be an ongoing character of the people who inhabit this land. In the eighteenth century and earlier, it was the site for the peace treaty and oral constitution developed by the Haudenosaunee, or the great Six Nations of indigenous Americans who speak Iroquois. Their Great Law of Peace, also known as Gayanashagowa, the Iroquois treaty, came about through a mutual desire to avoid war and to live in peace. It was so effective that it informed North American colonists like Benjamin Franklin, who shared it with his peers, and it has been recognized by the United States as having influenced the colonists' revolutionary work. Revolution, innovation, ferment—these are the qualities that characterize the place where Len and TJ would have their teenage worldviews rocked.

As Len and TJ surveyed the sky around the house the evening before they saw the UFO, Len saw "fleeting faint flashes of a pink-orange glow inside a nearby cumulus cloud, as if something were hiding and surreptitiously moving along within the cottony fluffs."

Many years later, when Len watched Steven Spielberg's *Close Encounters of the Third Kind,* he was struck by a scene in which a UFO hides inside a cloud as it approaches a woman's house to abduct her child.

"The quick orangish flashes inside the clouds that Spielberg portrayed were distinctly and eerily similar, almost identical, to what I saw that night on TJ's garage roof," Len said. "In fact, Spielberg's depiction was so authentically accurate to me that I snuggled down deeper into my movie seat to better appreciate his informed and skillful directorial efforts."

Len described how the prediction made in jest to his father—that he was going to look for a UFO—ironically came true.

"On the night we saw the UFO, four of us settled into our sleeping bags on the front lawn of TJ's house," he said.

At first, Len's friends goofed around and even played a trick on him. One of them focused a flashlight beam onto different parts of the lawn in quick dizzying bursts. "What's that?" they'd call out, feigning fear. "It's a UFO beam!" someone warned. Len finally caught them, laughed about the friendly joke they'd played on him, and in time the boys fell asleep. But Len stayed awake and gazed at the starry night sky.

"My eyes widened at about 2:00 A.M., when I saw a huge orange sphere with fiery flames fly into my view, emerging over the edge of the garage roof. It slowly floated—'glided' may be a better word—parallel to the horizon, with no downward trajectory whatsoever. It was silent, no sound at all. I've always described it as approximately the size of a high full moon, and it had a little white star-sized orb following frantically, seemingly abandoned, in its trail.

"Its shape was spherical in the front, with perhaps a slight tapering off toward the rear. It could've been acorn-shaped, with the larger end leading the way, but its true form was somewhat obscured by the brilliant flames. The flames, primarily red, orange, and yellow, started just behind the rounded orangish front and ended near the back, forming a flaring fiery tail. The completely silent object was moving so slowly, so deliberately, that I never had the sense the flames were caused by atmospheric friction of any kind. This was not a meteorite or free-falling piece of space debris. It seemed more as though the object had an internal problem, a chemical or material fire of some kind, and the little white orb had been left behind outside, following and trying to help, maybe maneuvering to get back inside.

"My recollection is, and I've thought and calculated long and hard about this, that it was traveling at an altitude of about two hundred feet—maybe less—and it seemed no more than thirty yards away from us horizontally. It was close, breathtakingly close. It appeared from the west-northwest and traveled in an east-southeasterly direction.

"I was astonished," he said, "It was spectacular."

Len kicked off his sleeping bag and shouted everyone awake.

"TJ later told me that when he first opened his eyes, the UFO looked like it was stopped in the sky right above him. As the object slowly passed by, probably fifteen seconds after my first sight, I ran without really thinking toward the front door of the house. Some good-citizen instinct seized me, and I was going to phone the police to report it. But as I approached the door, a calm, rational thought entered in my mind: *Stop. What's the point? Turn around and continue watching. Enjoy it.*

"And so I did. I was mesmerized as this UFO slowly continued its blazing way until it was out of view. The entire sighting lasted approximately thirty seconds, possibly a bit longer. I savored the sight of that moon-sized orange ball of flames floating deliberately and leisurely through the sky, like a cosmic torch, a beacon illuminating the darkness."

During the span of about six hours, the very period in

which Len and his friends saw their UFO, more than thirty
people in nearby towns and villages reported sightings. Their
descriptions, except for one, were consistent and similar to
what Len and his friends saw. The Upstate New York UFOs
of the summer of 1967 constitute a "UFO flap." A flap occurs
when UFOs have been reported by different people at different times within a short time span and at different locations
within the same geographical region.

These reports were made to the local sheriff's offices and
then reported in several different articles within ten days
by the *Rochester Democrat and Chronicle* and other news outlets. Of those who witnessed the UFO that Len and his friends
saw, two were Brockport policemen and two others were
Monroe County sheriff's deputies. One article specifically
named seven employees of the Lucidol Division at Geneseo
in Livingston County, who witnessed the same UFO that Len
saw. One of the Brockport witnesses was police officer Dave
Martens, who was Len's basketball coach and physical education teacher. He worked for the police department during
the summers.

The sighting that was not consistent with the other reports was that of a park security guard named Sidney Zipkin.
While Zipkin was on night duty, four hours before Len's sighting, he came upon a "mysterious craft in the parking lot" off
North Main Street in the town of Churchville, which is ten
miles from Brockport. Zipkin turned his truck headlights
on the craft and then saw "two midget-like men, dressed
in shiny, black uniforms, run past the truck and board the
saucer."[3] When the *Democrat and Chronicle* first reported
the flap, Zipkin's was the first sighting to be reported. Al-

though the report seemed dubious, apparently police and reporters in the 1960s took them seriously enough to write up the report and send it to Washington, DC, to the National Investigations Committee on Aerial Phenomena (NICAP). The newspaper report, unsurprisingly, emphasized the ludicrous nature of his story, yet also noted that Zipkin's supervisor said he was a good employee. Zipkin was well aware that his report was unbelievable.

"You can laugh at what I'm telling you—in fact, I used to laugh myself when people said they saw these things," the newspaper quoted Zipkin, "but I saw this with my own eyes and I swear to God as a witness that I saw what I saw."[4]

A few days later, the *Democrat and Chronicle* reported on NICAP's initial review of the flap. The headline read, "UFO Reports Investigated" with a subhead reading "Zipkin Is Doubted." The article states that "Zipkin's celebrated flying-saucer report has been sent to Washington, for scrutiny by top officials of the National Investigations Committee on Aerial Phenomena (NICAP). But indications are that his story . . . lacks credibility."

The article also referred to the sightings of other aerial phenomena by Len and multiple witnesses: "The NICAP placed more credibility in a recurring report that a UFO passed over the area about four hours after Zipkin reported his sighting to deputies. It [NICAP] said: 'The sighting of an object traversing the sky in an easterly direction at 2:08 a.m., August 1, has been confirmed by over 30 witnesses who viewed the object from widely-separated vantage points. The many independent descriptions of this brilliant object concur.' NICAP ruled out a bolide—an exploding or exploded meteor or meteorite."[5]

These reports and the subsequent investigation, all made within the later years of Project Blue Book, happened more than fifty-five years ago. Although only a little progress has been made in the academic, or visible and "public-facing," side of UFO studies since then, a few observations are clear from this example. First, almost everyone discounted the most absurd aspects of the phenomenon, represented by Zipkin's report. When officials received reports that conformed almost identically with other witnesses, they tended to lend credibility to the event. But when Zipkin declared he saw a craft with little people inside, they ridiculed it and rejected it. The only difference in content was that Zipkin reported a parked object and little men.

Additionally, the psychological states of the witnesses were peripheral to the NICAP investigation. It was the newspaper reporters who asked Zipkin how he "felt" about his sighting and the event.

"Were you drinking Monday night?" a reporter asked.

"No, I am a teetotaler," Zipkin replied.

"What did you do after work?"

"Went right home to bed."

"Did you sleep well?"

"Believe me, I stayed awake for a long, long time thinking about this, and then I had a bad sleep," Zipkin said.

I asked Len how *he* felt about the sighting. He explained his psychological reaction to the events in two parts. First, what he recalled he felt at the time it happened, and, second, how he feels about it today.

"My feelings and thoughts during the sighting were myriad, synapse-igniting, and contradictory. Of course, I was deeply aware of the super-synchronicity of the UFO's appearance considering the recent events, namely, the strange activity in the sky the night before, telling my father I was going to look for flying saucers that very night, and busting the flashlight-beam pranksters. Surely, some poet might read justice and vindication into the UFO's appearance that evening. But even as a teenager, I thought it was inappropriately egotistical of me to think this UFO had anything specifically to do with me. It had to be mere chance, a coincidence, right?

"And yet, the way this sighting made me feel was personal. I'll tell you the truth, because maybe it can help the research, possibly it has some bearing on the investigatory shift toward the experiencer's consciousness instead of on the materiality of the craft. When the UFO first appeared that night, blazing like a cannonball shot from a different dimension, it practically screamed to me without words, 'Behold, it's all true; here we are, from elsewhere, outside of your reality.'"

Len also discussed something that is a consistent pattern in reports of ongoing experiencers. It is the *knowing* that comes to them, like an external input. Experiencer's often will know that something relating to a UFO will happen, and they will receive a thought or an inclination to do something, like look up at the sky or know that a person will bring up the topic. Len experienced this moment while he thought he was going to perform the civic duty of reporting the sighting to the police. The *knowing* stopped him.

"I've wondered often about that moment when I ran off in a do-gooder's reaction to report the incident," he said.

"I had turned my back on the sighting, a phenomenon I'd

hoped to see for years, when a calming, gentle thought came over me, urging me to stop the fool's errand, turn around, and savor the view. From where did such a thought causing a dramatic abrupt change in action come?"

Len felt, but does not know for certain, that this sighting was personal and *for him*. Experiencers often report feelings that the sightings, even mass sightings, are somehow very personal to them, like a personal message. On some occasions experiencers feel that the encounter is an intrusion of privacy and describe it as eerie, as did TJ, who felt that he was being observed the night before through his window.

Often, researchers focus on certain aspects of a sighting yet leave out other data, such as the NICAP researchers who conferred credibility to the sightings that appeared to be aerial and light-infused crafts but deemed Zipkin's report of the beings and grounded saucer-shaped craft not credible. The field of ufology has been characterized by two general camps, which sometimes overlap. One camp includes those who believe that UFOs are mechanical, or "nuts and bolts," driven by travelers from another planet, like humans but with more advanced spaceships. Another camp links UFOs with new religious movements and consciousness. Recently, researchers have begun to consider more data, even that which is weirder than just spacecraft from another planet.

Len, who experienced the UFO flap that Zipkin had also witnessed, had disbelieved Zipkin's report, but, considering contemporary reports of UFOs, he now thinks there's a distinct possibility Zipkin may have been telling the truth.

"When I read his account a couple days after witnessing our UFO, I scoffed," he said.

"Even I, a card-carrying UFO nut who'd just witnessed a spectacular sighting, didn't believe Zipkin, and of course, no one else did, either. As I look back at the newspaper clippings, what Zipkin said, that two small-sized beings in black suits boarded a cigar-shaped craft at 10:15 P.M. in Churchville Park on July 31, 1967, is so close, so typical of the hundreds of accounts we've learned about and studied in the last six decades of UFO research, that it frankly sounds more real than fiction.

"Since there are countless reports of UFOs that change shape and appearance in flight, over time, to various people, it is not inconceivable that what Zipkin saw and what we saw a few hours later could've been the same UFO transformed into a different look."

As it turns out, Zipkin's life after his UFO sighting included serious criminal activity and even jail time. While this may hurt Zipkin's credibility, it is still the case that he made the first report in a series of reports by credible and unrelated witnesses. Although NICAP stated publicly that it didn't like what he reported, Zipkin stood by it.

One problem that confronts people who see UFOs and those who study sightings is that often people report seeing very different things. Since the scientific method requires the repetition of results in order to build knowledge, this element of UFO reports disqualifies the study of UFOs from traditional scientific research. A case in Florida reported by an attorney, Rey Hernandez, and his wife, Dulce, involved one sighting that resulted in two very different interpretations. Rey, who had been an atheist, witnessed an electric object buzz around his house and heal his ill pet dog. He described the object as a ball of plasma. Dulce also witnessed the same object. But she identified it as an angel. She is Roman Catholic.[6] Numerous sightings reveal a pattern in which UFOs don't appear the same to people who are involved in the same event.

Jacques Vallée notes with respect to the absurdity of the phenomena, "I think we are dealing with something that is both technological and psychic and seems to be able to manipulate other dimensions. This is neither wishful thinking nor personal speculation on my part. It's a conclusion that comes from interviewing critical witnesses, and then listening to what they have to say."[7]

A researcher who is also a scientist and an experiencer, who prefers to remain anonymous, notes that media reports tend to ignore the absurd elements of UFO sightings.

"I'm not sure what these experiences mean," he said, "and often it seems that I almost forget that they happened, but one thing for certain is that this stuff is way weirder than publicly acknowledged. If one includes all of the data and redacts nothing, I don't know how you can make the conclusion that it's extraterrestrial—meaning a regular biological being from another planet. Either we are incredibly biased to the point of stupidity, or this phenomenon can manipulate and control our beliefs and thoughts. I'm not dismissing the possibility of *Star Trek* space travelers, either biological or robotic, or artificial intelligence (AI), but that certainly isn't how I would characterize the things that I have experienced."[8]

The public reception of the experiencer's report often shapes how, and even if, the experiencer remembers the event. This includes responses from the experiencer's immediate family, friend group, and colleagues, and then media about the event if it had been reported. In Len's case, since the UFO was witnessed by his friends, his peer group reinforced his experience. But it was through subsequent and coincidental research into a subject completely different from the topic that he validated he had been part of something large that included many people.

"I told my father all about the UFO, the orange glow, the flames, the white orb following in its trail. I showed him news reports as they slowly trickled in. He took it all in, and I figured he was fully up to speed on this exciting story," he said.

"That summer, I was taking driver's education, and one of our assignments was to go through newspaper reports of car accidents in order to try to determine ways they might've been prevented. Searching through a stack of old newspapers, I found an article about the UFO incident that I'd missed before. It was headlined GENESEO MEN REPORT UFO, from the August 4, 1967, *Rochester Democrat and Chronicle*, page 12. In it, a witness states, 'It had an orangish-yellow glow. It had a white light in the tail,'" he said.

"This was the only article, the only other witness who saw, noticed, and reported the little white starlike orb following in the UFO's tail. I showed it to my dad, who was a professor of economics at SUNY Brockport and a former World War II counterintelligence officer. He read it, slowly looked up at me, and said, 'Now, I believe you.'"

Len had no idea that his father had doubted his original report. "I realized then and there," he said, "that persuading people of the reality of strange events was a tricky business. I did not doubt what I saw. But naively, I did not expect so many people to doubt me. People are wedded to their world-views."

Sight is an obvious theme within UFO reports, as they often begin with a sighting. Not only do people see something they cannot fit into their worldviews, but just being in the vicinity where others have had a sighting sometimes initiates a shift in perspective among some people. Jeffrey Kripal has called this shift in perspective a "flip" moment, a moment when one's perspective on life, reality, and the cosmos just flips, and one finds oneself inhabiting "a reversal of perspective, a new real."

"I do not know how, what it was, or why it was, but my UFO sighting forever changed me," Len said. "It was my first dramatic transcendent experience. The personal-touch synchronicity of it, whether intended or strictly coincidental, has stayed with me to this day, igniting my curiosity, reshaping my worldview. It also opened my eyes to the inescapable fact that government authorities and maybe even science were either lying to us about UFOs or they were sorely incompetent. It made me more wary, cynical, and distrustful of pronouncements by our society's institutional authorities."

Another event that "flipped" Len's perspective occurred after he had a chance encounter in the 1970s with Archbishop Fulton Sheen, the man who appeared to millions of people through their television sets to remind them that "life is worth living." Following that, his experience of life deepened and transformed. His ongoing conversion included a vision of Sheen and extraordinarily vivid dreams.

10

THE DREAM NETWORK

Dreamscapes, Visions, and Lucid Dreams

Who looks outside dreams; who looks inside awakes.

—ATTRIBUTED TO CARL JUNG

If the UFO encounter is like a window, as described by John Mack and Jacques Vallée, then Len had peered through this window and stepped into another, enchanted world. From this other world, he peered back and then climbed into the "real world" again. For a time, however, he existed in two worlds. While Len did not forget about his UFO encounter, it was certainly not at the forefront of his thoughts as a young man. He studied journalism and went on to become popular and successful in the media, in politics, and in the film industry of New York. He was part of a group of influential young professionals in the 1970s who worked hard and partied harder. The hedonistic high life, while enjoyable, was not sustainable for Len, and one day he provided himself with the circumstances that led to a wakeup call. A chance meeting figured prominently in this event.

In 1975, Len worked as an intern reporter for WROC-TV news in Rochester, New York. The news director of the station assigned Len to assist the lead reporter covering Fulton Sheen's return visit to Rochester to give a speech. Sheen had served as the bishop of Rochester from October 1966 to October 1969. Len was among a throng of other reporters with cameras, lights, and recording devices, ready to catch a glimpse of and possibly interview Sheen.

"Sheen entered the room. He was attired in a red robe over a black suit, as I recall, and was dutifully attended to by an entourage of church and hotel assistants. He dressed and strode like a king."

Len was prepared for the reporters to mob Sheen, but they didn't. He was amazed that the other reporters simply watched as Sheen walked by.

"No one asked for an interview. No one shouted out a question. My full-time reporter colleague had not yet arrived, so emboldened with a determination to get the story, I decided to approach Sheen. I gently touched him on the back of his shoulder just before he almost got away into the formal luncheon, and asked, 'Do you have a moment for Channel 8 News?'"

"I fully expected him to ignore my request and keep walking," Len said. "I felt the eyes of all the other 'real' reporters watching me. No doubt they'd snigger when Sheen either rejected or reprimanded me. But Archbishop Fulton J. Sheen stopped and turned around to look straight into my eyes. His blue eyes were piercing, like a hawk's, and he was serene amid the chaos of the media and his anxious entourage. He stood calm in the middle of the storm.

"'Of course,' he replied gently, graciously."

This event had a big impact on Len, whose upbringing was completely secular. He had never seen or talked with anyone associated with the Catholic hierarchy. His parents did not affiliate with any religion, nor were they spiritual. Yet this chance meeting of Sheen would prove to have an afterlife. When he saw Fulton Sheen again, it would be in a vision.

In the few short years since his brief encounter with Sheen, Len enjoyed more professional success. He served as a traveling state press secretary to the successful 1976 Jimmy Carter presidential campaign (Carter reported his own 1969 sighting of a UFO) and on Capitol Hill for Representative Andrew Maguire of New Jersey. In 1979, after wrapping up a stint as unit publicist for a successful low-budget horror movie (*Fear No Evil,* directed by Frank LaLoggia), Len was in New York City visiting friends and taking a break. "That was a bit of a lost weekend," Len admits. "I was overindulging in excess." Len recalls that after a week of hard partying and drinking, he found himself with an excruciatingly painful hangover.

In a state of soul desperation, Len reflected upon his life. He had been successful and believed that this track record would continue. He had friends. His parents were supportive. Yet he was alone, in a shabby hotel room, feeling despondent and without hope. Nothing terrible had led him to this recognition, other than depression from overdrinking and the realization that something was missing, that his life lacked meaning.

"I silently called out to the universe for help," he said. "A sense of calm quickly befell me, and for the first time in hours, I relaxed. Memories started to take shape, elbowing out the self-recriminations. I began to remember, for no apparent reason, in detail, the time I met Archbishop Fulton J. Sheen.

"*Why am I remembering this?* I thought. *I know nothing about Sheen, have paid no attention to his sermons. I don't believe in him, his religion, or, for that matter, in any religion.* But the reminiscences gave me brief respite from the storm, so I indulged them.

"And then, with my eyes closed, I saw in my mind's eye, my inner vision, a startling and clear image of Sheen's face as I'd seen him in Rochester, in full color, smiling kindly. This image of Sheen's shining face slowly rolled upward inside my meditative field of vision and rose higher and higher until out of view.

"*Wow,* I thought, *that was intense,*" Len continued. "I'd never before seen such a clear, photographic-quality meditative image of anything in my mind's eye, and I'd certainly never seen one in such vivid color."

I asked Len if he thought that this was a dream. He described it in more detail and called it a vision.

"This was not a dream. I was fully awake," he said. "The inner vision of Sheen's face and the memory of our meeting soothed me, although I didn't attach any deep spiritual significance to it," he said. "I found the incident curious, not religious, a strictly secular recollection of a past event. The remembrance of the kindness Sheen had shown me, and the strikingly unique nature of this colorful vision eased the turmoil of my existential crisis that dark night."

He recalled that the detail and vividness of the image

was something unusual. "I'd never before or since experienced such a vivid, dreamish vision during a waking meditative state." More unusual, however, was what happened a few hours after the image appeared to him.

"The very next morning, sitting on the subway, I scanned the front page of *The New York Times*. Flipping it over to the stories below the fold, I read the bold headline: ARCHBISHOP SHEEN, WHO PREACHED TO MILLIONS OVER TV, IS DEAD AT 84. He died in his Upper East Side apartment the very night of my vision."

Fulton Sheen died in his private chapel on the night of December 9, 1979. He died while praying in front of the Blessed Sacrament, which in Catholic and Orthodox Christian traditions is the consecrated wafer, called the Eucharist. It is believed by practitioners of these religions to be the presence of Jesus Christ. When Len learned that Sheen had passed away on the very night of his vision, during the hours of his own "dark night of the soul," he was shocked. He describes being changed instantly.

"I was struck by a deep realization of otherness, of otherworldliness. Reality shifted for me as the realization of this 'aha' synchronicity took hold. I vibrated at a rate different from the other passengers and the subway car's cold metal motion. Other riders seemed blurred, out of focus. It was *Twilight Zone*–ish. I don't know how else to describe it other than my entire essence vibrated at a distinctly different frequency from everyone and everything around me. The unthinkable question forced itself upon me: Had Sheen's spirit visited me?"

Years later, Len learned that the Catholic Church started

an investigation into the canonization of Fulton Sheen. While he did not and does not consider his experience with Sheen anything resembling a miracle, he felt he "owed it" to someone or something to report it in order to provide more background information on Sheen. He sent letters to the Catholic committee studying Sheen's potential canonization, and later, he published an essay about it in *Busted Halo,* a Catholic online periodical. It was this publication that he had sent to me and that got my attention. He prefaced it with the question: "Do you think there is a UFO connection here?" I read his story, found it charming, and sent it to my colleagues who organized the Rice University conference, the Archives of the Impossible. Len quickly acquired the nickname the "Fulton Sheen Guy" among some members of the group. What I thought was unique about Len's vision, other than the vision itself, was that he refused to conclude as to what it meant. Ultimately, he doesn't know what it means. Significantly, he credits it with being a foundational shift in his life's direction and ultimate spiritual journey. He does, however, speculate on possible meanings of the event.

"It seemed to me, if I were to venture a wild guess, that upon his death, Archbishop Fulton J. Sheen's spiritual energy, his consciousness, his soul may have erupted in a glorious shower of cosmic grace that was felt nearby in Manhattan by many people with whom he'd crossed paths. As with his broadcasts, he said goodbye with flair and style.

"How else to explain this? While it may be possible in a spiritual sense that Sheen's life force responded specifically to my plea for help, gave me comfort when I needed it as he left the material world, I truly think it had nothing to do with me. It's about the special nature of Sheen, his eccentric benevolence, perhaps the special nature of *his* God. I merely stumbled, hungover, into the trajectory of his transitioning spiritual essence."

My colleagues enjoyed Len's story. One of them asked, "But is this connected with a UFO?"

Many people who experience UFO events report unusual dreams and visions after the event and as ongoing phenomena. Often, they call these dreams visions, waking or lucid dreams, or vivid dreams. Sometimes they feel that their own sighting is like a dream, in that they can't remember it very well. They often question if the event happened, even when there were multiple witnesses and evidence such as radar reported by local airports. Sometimes they just forget it, and then the memory is activated by later events.

An example of this latter dreamlike characteristic linked to an encounter is illustrated by actor Kurt Russell's plane flight in 1997, which corresponded with the controversial Arizona UFO flap known as the Phoenix Lights. Unlike Len's UFO sighting, the Phoenix Lights, witnessed by thousands of people in Arizona, have never been officially proclaimed "unidentified," except to thousands of civilians who believe they witnessed something from another world. Were they flares, stealth aircraft, or something else? According to Russell, the weirdest part of the incident was the fact that he forgot about it.

Russell, a pilot, describes seeing unidentified lights and reporting them.

"I saw six lights over the airport in absolute uniform, in a V-shape. . . . I was just looking at them and I was coming in; we were maybe a half mile out. [His son] said, 'Pa, what are those lights?' Then I kind of came out of my reverie and I said, 'I don't know what they are.' He said, 'Are we okay here?' I said 'I'm gonna call,' and I reported it. They said, 'We don't show anything.'

"I said, 'Well, okay, I'm gonna declare it's unidentified, it's flying and it's six objects.' We landed, I taxied, dropped him off, took off, and went back to L.A.

"I never said a word; he never said a word. I never thought of it. Two years later, [his partner] Goldie [Hawn] is watching a television show when I came home. And the show is on UFOs. . . . And I'm kind of hearing the TV going. And I stopped and I started watching, and it was on that event. And that was the most viewed UFO event, over twenty thousand people saw that.

"I'm watching this and I'm feeling like Richard Dreyfuss in *Close Encounters of the Third Kind*. I go, 'What—why do I know this?' And it's not clear to me. And finally they said a general-aviation pilot reported it on landing.

"I never thought of it since then, and I said, 'That was me, that was me! Wait a minute, I'll go to my logbooks.' So I went to my logbooks and there was that flight, at that time, and I didn't mention anything about the UFO.

"The fascinating part of that, to me, was that it just went literally out of my head. And [my son] never mentioned it. Had I not seen the show I never would've thought of it again. That, to me, was the weird part."[1]

Russell experienced a "reverie" during the sighting, and then forgot about it. When he remembered it, he questioned how he could have forgotten it. As strange as it seems, this is a pattern that occurs with many UFO events, sightings, and dreams. Like dreams, these events seem to be difficult to remember.

Experiencers report dreams that are distinctive from their ordinary dreams. Dreams of UFOs, or alleged aliens, or dreams that follow UFO events seem to fall within a similar liminal category of consciousness. Generally, most people make a distinction between ordinary reality and dream reality, and they do not mix these up. However, what happens when dream reality seems to merge with waking reality in ways that seem impossible yet offer evidence of things that cannot be denied, such as dreams of future events or even dreams of meeting others who share the same dreamscape? In most instances, these types of dreams stretch the limits of contemporary Western scientific dream research, although there are notable exceptions. Anthropologist Amira Mittermaier explains that Sigmund Freud, for example, was aware of dreams that defied Western epistemological categories, and the work of science author and anthropologist Eric Wargo explains these dreams through contemporary frameworks of science and physics.[2]

Some types of dreams, like lucid dreams, have only recently showed up on the radar of current sleep research, whereas some communities, such as non-Western indigenous communities and Western esoteric traditions, have recognized and utilized these liminal states for more than centuries. Psychologist and sleep study researcher Jayne Gackenbach, who pioneered Western studies into lucid dreams, notes, "Whether we should consider it a paradoxical form of sleep or a paradoxical form of waking or something else entirely, it seems too early to tell. Terms like *sleep, waking,* and *dreaming* may be too crude to capture usefully the fine structure of consciousness. Our vocabulary for describing certain states of consciousness is still too undeveloped."[3]

In a discussion of the central place that dreams have in the history of esotericism, Dr. Aaron French notes, "Modern theosophy and anthroposophy texts state very clearly that the goal of initiation is to bring the realm of dreaming—i.e., unconscious or spirit realm—into one's waking reality. In other words, to merge waking and dreaming states in one's ordinary life; that is the goal according to these esoteric texts."[4]

French, who specializes in the works of the prominent teacher of esotericism Rudolf Steiner, discussed how Steiner placed important emphasis on dreams as they related to spiritual initiations:

[During initiation] the possibility arises for the individual to go through a certain portion of the night in a conscious condition. His physical body sleeps as usual, but a part of his sleep-condition becomes animated by significant dreams. These are the first heralds of his entrance into the higher worlds. Gradually, he leads his experiences over into his ordinary consciousness. He then sees astral beings in his entire environment, even here in the room between the chairs, or out in the woods and meadows.[5]

These reflections on the function of dreams within esoteric spiritual initiations shed light on the experiences that many people have after they see or have been in the vicinity of a UFO. Not only are these not ordinary dreams but ordinary people, I presume, would not be comfortable with the appearance of astral beings in their living rooms. This is an experience I would choose to avoid. Time and again people report dreams that they insist are not ordinary. Gray Man, Jose, and Kary Mullis all insist that what they experienced were not dreams but somehow waking visions or something that occurred in waking life. Could Gray Man and Mullis have been experiencing initiations similar to what Steiner discusses? Jose, who sees his experiences within a religious and spiritual worldview, is not vexed at all by these spontaneous appearances. They go with the territory of being awake. Although he doesn't ignore the appearance of UFOs, he doesn't really pay extra attention to them, either. Beyond the Western esoteric framework of dream interpretation, many indigenous traditions and certain traditional religions support a link between nonordinary dream states and transformative spiritual experiences.

Gackenbach explored sophisticated dream epistemologies in the centuries-old traditions of indigenous Australian culture called the Alcheringa, roughly translated as the "Dreamtime" or the "Dreaming," and within some traditions of Tibetan Buddhism.[6] In a series of conversations about dreams, Tibetan Buddhist Lama Lhanang Rinpoche and Jayne Gackenbach discussed intersections between Western dream research and Tibetan Buddhist dream yoga. The Western approach, Gackenbach notes, tends to "pathologize these states of consciousness." Just as current dream science reveals that brain states during sleep correspond to different types of dreams, Lama Rinpoche identified the varieties of dreams within his tradition.

He identified dreams about everyday life, dreams in the early morning that tend to be more significant than ordinary dreams, and dreams in which a person connects with "the spirit world." He said that these latter types of dreams, which are less frequent than the other types of dreams, can be magical or terrifying. Rinpoche also said that consciousness is a continuum, and that waking reality is another form of a dream. He also likened magical dreams to the state of mind of being an artist. If one is very involved in art, this was akin to the magical dreams of Tibetan dream yoga, he said.

"Through the dreams you can go there, you can go and receive the teachings of the five Buddha families," he said. "Through art you can contact the Buddha worlds." He explained that he had a dream when he was a child that he would one day hold the president of the United States' hand. When he was grown, this dream came true. He described how, after shaking hands with the president, he wondered, *Wow, my dream came true.*

"How much do you think dreams tell the future?" Gackenbach asked.

"I think some people have cleaned their minds. Their minds are light and they become psychic and they see things that are going to happen," he said.

The conversation continued to the topic of flying in one's dream. Experiencers often feel that they levitate, either out of their rooms, into crafts, or to other places altogether. "If you do this you need a teacher," Rinpoche said.

"Some [people] can go anywhere in the universe and they can learn things from dreams, and they can bring this back. Buddha talked about this 2,500 years ago; there is no distance, everything is connected," he said.

"If we fly in a plane for five thousand years it is far away, but if you try this in meditation, you get there in one second, so there's no distance. Today, there's no distance. You can be going to bed and you see a person [on your phone] and they are just waking up for breakfast. There is no distance."

Rinpoche's use of technology as a frame for dreams is significant. In this view, dreams are an interface between worlds. In the Alcheringa, or the Dreamtime concept shared by the great variety of indigenous Australians, the most efficacious of their dreamers travel in dreams or in dreamlike states. In my initial research into the Alcheringa, I read the works of nonindigenous anthropologists, as this is the typical way in which Western people acquire knowledge about indigenous systems and lifeways. What struck me was the prodigious efforts that researchers took to try to translate the term "Alcheringa." One researcher wrote three pages of etymological research to do justice to the concept. The impression I got was that this was a system that was so complex that anthropologists had a hard time understanding it, and then once they did, their efforts to translate it into writing failed. The system defied reductive forms of language. Of course, the best source for understanding the Alcheringa is an indigenous Australian.

In Tyson Yunkaporta's book *Sand Talk*, he explains the Dreaming:

I use many other terms that I don't particularly like, such as "Dreaming" (which is a mistranslation and misinterpretation), because a lot of the old people I respect, and who have passed knowledge on to me, use these words. It's not my place to disrespect them by rejecting their vocabulary choices. I know and they know what they mean, so we might as well just use those labels. In any case, it is almost impossible to speak in English without them, unless you want to say, "suprarational interdimensional ontology endogenous to custodial ritual complexes" every five minutes. So "Dreaming" it is.[7]

Yunkaporta's explanation, like Lama Rinpoche's, links dimensions with reference to ontologies of space-time. Mittermaier, in her book about Egyptian Muslim dreaming, also references the "suprarational" aspect of the dreamscape. "I want to call into question the presumption that all dreams are inherently linked to the psyche."[8] The idea that there could possibly be dream states that are independent of human minds is counterintuitive for many people, except for those who study people's dreams. Mittermaier goes on to cite the work of other scholars who have come to similar conclusions, such as Vincent Crapanzano. "Much of what we in the West call psychological and locate in some sort of internal space ('in the head,' 'in the mind,' 'in the brain,' 'in consciousness,' 'in the psyche') is understood in many cultures in manifestly nonpsychological terms and located in 'other spaces.'"[9]

These other spaces can be uncanny, like in the instance

of an indigenous Australian woman who dreamed of her father in a cemetery. In her dream he described how he was disturbed in his place of rest, the cemetery, by her actions during a recent social gathering that involved gambling. The woman's father wasn't upset with her about gambling, but he was upset that she utilized his memory as a means to acquire luck during the session. In her dream, she crouched and drew in the sand at the cemetery yard. When she woke up in the morning, she had sand and leaves from the yard on her gown and in her hands.[10]

An archaeologist I know works closely with one Australian tribe and described how, within the tribe with which he was familiar, there were levels of initiation, somewhat like esoteric societies in the West. He explained that certain people were given or initiated into different lore. What happens in the Dreaming was as important as what happens in daily life and significantly impacts it. Because the Dreaming is passed along through oral tradition, just as is most of Tibetan dream yoga, what can be known to outsiders is limited and limited to sources who have contact with initiates. "We know the difference between [normal dreams and special dreams] but do not tell anyone about the special dreams, except [the] old men."[11]

Some initiations involve dream travel, like the example related by Lama Rinpoche about Tibetan Buddhist dreamers who go to places and bring things back. The things they bring back include knowledge, and as for the indigenous Australians, they bring back information that they share with each other and sometimes store in their material art. They place hidden knowledge in the form of code in their art, to be deciphered by people from neighboring tribes or by their youths. On other occasions, they conduct dream meetings with other initiates. Initiates remember what is said in these meetings and carry this into their waking lives.

"The special dreams characteristically were highly salient and realistic and involved many senses," the archaeologist said. "They were said to be so vivid that the dreamer could 'see, hear, and feel the rain' of the dream. Another man explained the difference as being very difficult to differentiate between reality in the everyday world and the reality of the special dream. Some said that they were aware of being in the dream. These dreams fall into the category of lucid dreaming, where one is aware that one is dreaming, and the events are vividly depicted. They are so vivid, in fact, that they seem more real than waking reality," he said.

"One of the community leaders is a good friend, and she described how her son was going out to participate in 'Lore time,' and the night before he went out, he had a dream in which he was flying around the landscape and saw a cave that he already knew of, and the cave was lit up with bright light, so he flew there and entered. He entered the cave and there was art and painted symbols moving on the walls with all the light, and at the back of the cave was an old man with war paint on and he was performing a dance, and this old man was singing in an unknown language and tried to teach the boy how to perform the dance he was doing. And then the very next day, while learning the ceremonial protocols for the Lore, an elder taught all the kids a particular dance, to encourage flying in dreams(!), and it was the exact same dance that the old man in the cave taught him in his dream.

"Most aspects of the Dreaming are forbidden to be revealed to outsiders unless they go through the Lore, so it can be difficult to penetrate, and I learn something new every time I head out into the field. But within some ceremonies known to me, a trancelike state is often sought because of the ceremony, which is often accompanied with a belief that advice can be received by spirits who are attracted to these situations. Tangentially, different behaviors can be considered as protocols. Such as an old man telling me that he will go out to remote locations to be in silence."[12]

Significantly, the Alcheringa is not a philosophy apart from daily waking life; it is inextricable from material waking reality. Dreamtime inhabits waking life. Waking life is informed by the Dreamtime. Len Filppu has experienced several vivid dreams, and they are more akin to Dreamtime events and Tibetan dream yoga practices than the tools he has found within his secular life's toolbox.

LEN'S DREAMS

"These vivid dreams are strikingly unlike the jumbled jangle of my other ordinary every-night kind of dreams," Len said. "Each is in resplendent color, wakes me up awed and thinking, and they're as memorable as the anomalous experiences I've had in everyday reality."

Len also clarified that he never practiced dreamwork or dream journaling and never tried to summon vivid dreams. They "came of their own accord," he said, "just as have my anomalous episodes." In the following vivid dream, Len

receives a message from a deceased man who asks him to convey a message to a stranger. It is a lucid dream.

"There are countless tales of salvation, redemption, and spiritual progress in the rooms of recovery, where I first met John about four decades ago," Len said.

"Quick-witted and funny as hell, John had been a military officer, a successful businessman, and a gifted musician. He was committed to his own sobriety and to helping others get established in clean and sober living. A bit of a rascal, John was a frequent and sought-after speaker at fellowship events. In common language, he was a pillar of the recovery community.

"And so it was a blow to all who knew him to learn he died on December 4, 2021."

Len relates how two nights after John's death, he dreamed about him. Like his vision of Fulton Sheen, the dream was in full color and very vivid and seemed more important than an ordinary dream.

"John's presence came to me in this dream, came to my bedside and awakened me so I'd pay attention to something urgent he needed to share. He seemed in a hurry, like he didn't have much time, and really wanted to wake me up. Of course, I was asleep. But inside my vivid dream state, I woke up alert and focused on John.

"He said/communicated that there was a man who attends a recovery meeting I sometimes attend who needed to know that John had not abandoned him. John had just started working with him on sobriety and had promised to contact him but hadn't, because, well, he died. John needed to close the loop with his new sponsee. That's the kind of dedication John had to helping others.

"In my vivid dream, I understood John's determination to make sure this person he'd been working with did not think John didn't care or that John's methodology for sobriety was bogus. People can die if the program—the lifeline newcomers and old-timers alike rely upon—malfunctions or appears to be a false mirage.

"I asked John, through thought, *Who is this person?* He communicated a name, but that name did not register with me. He then communicated, *The guy with the strange hat.* I thought of the people often in that room, and visualized a guy I had earlier thought—completely to myself—wore a stylish but odd-ish hat. In other words, John seemed to know the inside of my thoughts. He knew of my previous uncommunicated notion that this guy wore a chapeau uncommon to our area's norm, and he used that 'inside knowledge' to help me identify the correct person.

"*I know who it is,* I communicated, and John seemed to know we'd identified the right man. As though this errand was now completed and he had many other stops to make, John quickly flew off and up, away from me, his image vaporizing as he departed.

"I woke up. It was dawn.

"This vivid dream stunned me. It felt like it was a true communication from John to me. I was surprised, because although I'd known and loved John for several decades, I wouldn't have expected him to contact me. He was viscerally closer to many others in the community. But as I kept thinking, maybe he connected with me because I sometimes went to the same meeting as this hat man.

"I told my wife about the dream. She agreed it was remarkable. I told her I must attend that meeting that very morning, while the feeling of the dream still permeated my consciousness. I needed to see if the guy with the hat was there.

"Inside the room before the meeting started, several friends were gathered in small groups drinking coffee and chatting. I heard someone report to others that John had died. I saw the man with the odd hat. He paid attention to this comment about John's death. He said something aloud but more to himself, something like, 'Oh, he died; that explains it.'

"I immediately introduced myself to this man and invited him outside for a private talk. I told him the story of my vivid dream, how much John wanted to connect with him, and to make sure he knew John's lack of communication was due not to negligence but to life's most inescapable reason.

"The man was deeply moved, relieved, to hear my report. Yes, he'd wondered what had happened to John, why he hadn't heard from him as promised. He thanked me for sharing this vivid dream with him and indicated that it all made sense to him, no matter the tale's extraordinary nature."

I thanked Len for the dream reports he sent. Each report had a profound impact on me. A few days after I had asked Len about his dreams, he sent me a follow-up note.

"Diana, I didn't remember the date of John's death so I had to look it up. My dream about him was a couple days after his death. Surprisingly, that puts it exactly one year from the day I began writing to you about my John dream.

Unwittingly, I began writing about his dream visitation on the exact one-year anniversary of it happening."

＊　＊　＊

If Len's dream had been just one event, it would be cause for wonder. And that would be the end of it. His dream, however, is one of many that he has experienced, each one as wondrous as the next, and distinguished from his ordinary dreams. Additionally, dreams like these constitute a trend within a sizable group of people who report seeing UFOs, and certainly among the people featured in the present study. The dreams contain repeated features like lucidity, in that the dreamer believes he or she is awake. They are colorful and rich in detail. They are often precognitive in that they contain information that is later found to be true. Like Len's dream of John, they often contain a message that is meant to be delivered to another person. These dreams often contain information to which the dreamer shouldn't have access under normal circumstances. For example, Len was not aware that John was counseling the man with the odd hat. In some dream reports, experiencers report that they meet with other people in "dream meetings" and collaborate. One scientist I knew said that he and colleagues had a similar technique of going to places in their dream states to acquire knowledge that helps them solve problems in their work. A technopreneur told me that she and her colleagues would meet in their dreams and discuss code and carry on the conversation the next day.

Len has created a successful business, family, community,

and writing life. He told me that he calls his mystic journey "Len's Magical Mystery Tour, with a tip of the hat to the Beatles." As a child he asked to see a UFO, and he did. It seemed to him that his request was answered. That event opened his mind to other worlds.

"Sure, I'd love to understand what it all means," Len said, "but I'm okay with living with the mystery."

Len did tell me that the reason he is sharing his story, at the risk of rejection and ridicule, is in hopes that more scholars, scientists, and journalists will explore these aspects of human experience with more vigor, open-mindedness, and honesty.

These experiences eventually led Len to a conversion from atheism. To what did he convert? One could call Len's form of spirituality a variety of "spiritual but not religious," a phrase that has been used to describe a growing development in North American religious landscapes at the turn of the twentieth century. As scholars of religion have argued, the apparent transhistorical nature of this phrase belies the ways in which people's beliefs have been formed through ongoing tensions between religious and secular communities. Could Len's experiences represent something altogether different—historically situated, no doubt, but indicative of latent esoteric truths, of which a kid like Len might have no inkling in Brockport, New York, in the 1960s? The experiences told in the pages of this book indicate that the answer to this question is *yes*, and the UFO is the window through which these truths are often perceived.

CONCLUSION

The End of an Allegory

As I finished this book, Simone and I were in a feverish race to keep up with the rapid pace of developments in AI in order to keep her chapter current. By the time this book is published, no doubt the entire landscape of our lives will have completely changed due to the exponential rate of change in that field. In a world of exponential technological growth, I don't think books will be able to keep pace, at least not in the way they are currently being published. As I finish the final edits to this manuscript on March 29, 2023, a new paper has been published about the amazing capacities of GPT4 (Chat GTP 4). Simone and her cohorts would view this era as the time when we meet the alien, the extraterrestrial from out of space-time.

Be that as it may, I've provided, as best I could, the state of UFO research as it pertains to witnesses and what I have learned from UFO subcultures. If you picked up this book to learn about UFOs and you had no previous knowledge about them then you were probably shocked, like I had been, to find that witness testimonies reveal that UFO contact events are not like they are depicted in most media representations, and not what is shown on social media sites. Instead, UFO contact events include supernatural and paranormal elements and influence people's lives in ways that reorient them at the level of their values and core beliefs.

Additionally, a deep dive into the lives of experiencers reveals an initiation into a new life—one characterized by vivid and lucid dreams, altered states of reality, the presence of UFOs and supernatural beings like angels, as well as the presence of a network of information that many experiencers believe they can access.

Another theme that emerges, which is perhaps the strangest, is the presence of groups of people who have managed the public narrative of UFOs in the United States. These groups, whom I've termed The Invisibles, are enigmatic but very real. There are also groups of scientists who have studied UFOs and who have passed on the information they've learned through an oral tradition, not unlike the oral traditions found in esoteric philosophies. Some UFO data is stored in human bodies and minds; it is not written down. This tradition is similar in many ways to religious traditions such as those found in Tibetan Buddhism and in the Western tradition.

As a way to make sense of my research, I turned to the philosophical text called "The Allegory of the Cave," which occupies a small space in Plato's *Republic*. It became a guide and provided a framework for my understanding of UFO cultures and communities. Plato, whose teacher Socrates was murdered by his government for transmitting esoteric, gnostic knowledge to Greek youth, wrote about the transmission of this knowledge as an allegory. The more I considered this genre choice—the allegorical form—the more I recognized that this might have been necessary due to the context of Plato's life and experience (and as a scholar of religion, as a matter of course we place historical texts within their cultural contexts). I learned from my friends in philosophy that Socrates's group of students lived in trauma after their teacher's murder. They were a community under duress and the treatment of Socrates was a warning to them. It made sense that Plato would use the allegorical form to convey Socrates's knowledge to those who could understand it. It was a secret code and a means of transmission to others who had to remain invisible or suffer a similar fate.

The theme of invisibility with respect to esoteric knowledge seems to be central to UFO subcultures. Allen Hynek referenced the scientists of the early modern era, who called themselves The Invisible College and worked under a cloak of secrecy under an ever-present danger of persecution, torture, and death. He used the term for his own cohort of scientists, The Invisible College. The Allegory spoke to these aspects of UFO cultures, which is why I returned to it again and again. It lives as a gift from past initiates to future philosophers. Perhaps a day will come, and soon, when UFO knowledge and its pursuit will be free and unfettered by the cloak-and-dagger atmosphere of the previous century.

ACKNOWLEDGMENTS

I would like to acknowledge the people who have inspired me and helped me throughout the process of writing this book. I am grateful to those who have shared their experiences. They are Simone, Jose, Iya, Len, Patricia, and Gray Man. Each of their stories, and their lives, have profoundly influenced me and I am humbled that they've trusted me to share part of their extraordinary lives. I am thankful to my husband, children, mother, and my brothers. They are, and have always been, supportive of me and my work. My colleagues have been invaluable, and I am lucky to know them, not just because they are brilliant and I learn a lot from them but also because they make me laugh. They include Jeffrey Kripal, Jacques Vallée, Garry Nolan, Hussein Ali Agrama, David B. Metcalfe, Greg Bishop, Whitley Strieber, Josh Boone, Leslie Kean, various people in The Invisible College, James Iandoli, Aaron French, Matthew Roberts, and the new friends I've made who live in Australia. I was influenced by the ideas and writings of Marie Mutsuki Mockett and Josh the Archaeologist. I am indebted to the senior Martu woman who allowed me to write about certain Dream Lore of her culture, and the Martu man who has been initiated into the Lore. I also want to thank Matthew Gruchow for providing essays instrumental in framing parts of the book. I also want to thank my childhood friends who saved my sanity and my life on a few occasions, including Lynn Wilbur, Thomas Master, and Lilian Ortiz. My current editor, Joel Fotinos, and my agent, Giles Anderson, deserve special thanks. I am always grateful for the help and guidance of my former editor, Cynthia Read. I also would like to acknowledge the influence on this book of Tyler D. The research time frame overlaps with our work together and my present focus.

NOTES

Introduction

1. *American Cosmic* details the specific ways in which UFO belief is culti- vated and directed. See D. W. Pasulka, *American Cosmic: UFOs, Religion, Technology* (New York: Oxford University Press, 2019).

2. Office of the Director of National Intelligence. Preliminary Assessment: Un- identified Aerial Phenomena; June 25, 2021. Reports and Publications: 2021. https://www.dni.gov/index.php/newsroom/reports-publications/reports -publications-2021/item/2223-preliminary-assessment-unidentified-aerial -phenomena.

3. https://www.ourstrangeplanet.com/the-san-luis-valley/guest-editorials /jacques-vallee-interview/.

4. David C. Posthumus, *All My Relatives: Exploring Lakota Ontology, Be- lief, and Ritual*, New Visions in Native American and Indigenous Studies (Lincoln: University of Nebraska Press and The American Philosophical Society, 2018).

5. Sonya Atalay, William Lempert, David Delgado Shorter, and Kim Tall- Bear, "Indigenous Studies Working Group Statement," *American Indian Culture and Research Journal* 45, no. 1 (2021): 9–18.

6. Suzanne Kite, "'What's on the Earth Is in the Stars; and What's in the Stars Is on the Earth': Lakota Relationships with the Stars and Ameri- can Relationships with the Apocalypse," *American Indian Culture and Research Journal*, 42, no. 1 (2018): 29–49.

7. Jacques Vallée, *Invisible College: What a Group of Scientists Has Discov- ered About UFO Influence on the Human Race* (Charlottesville, NC: Anom- alist Books, 1975), 203–4.

Chapter 1: The Space Psychologist

1. Enrique Rivera, "William Shatner experienced profound grief in space. It was the 'overview effect,'" NPR, October 23, 2022. https://www.npr

.org/2022/10/23/1130482740/william-shatner-jeff-bezos-space-travel
-overview-effect.

2. Iya Whiteley and Olga Bogatyreva, *Toolkit for a Space Psychologist: To Support Astronauts in Exploration Missions to the Moon and Mars* (London: Cosmic Baby Books, 2018).

3. Frank White, *The Overview Effect: Space Exploration and Human Evolution* (Restin, VA: American Institute of Aeronautics: 2014).

4. Deana L. Weibel, "The Overview Effect and the Ultraview Effect: How Extreme Experiences in/of Outer Space Influence Religious Beliefs in Astronauts," *Religions* 11, no 8 (2020): 418.

5. "Links," Overview Institute. https://overviewinstitute.org/links/.

6. Weibel, "The Overview Effect and the Ultraview Effect."

7. D. B. Yaden, J. Iwry, Kelley J. Slack, Johannes C. Eichstaedt, Yukun Zhao, George E. Vaillant, Andrew B. Newberg, "The Overview Effect: Awe and Self-Transcendent Experience in Space Flight," *Psychology of Consciousness: Theory, Research, and Practice* 3, no. 1 (2016): 1–11.

8. Benjamin Walter, "To the Planetarium," in *On the Program of the Coming Philosophy, Selected Writings, Volume 1: 1913–1926*, ed. Marcus Bullock and Michael W. Jennings, transl. Rodney Livingstone (Cambridge, MA: Belknap Press, 1996): 103–10.

9. Weibel, "The Overview Effect and the Ultraview Effect," 11.

10. Ibid., 418.

11. Timothy Morton, *Hyperobjects: Philosophy and Ecology after the End of the World* (Minneapolis: University of Minnesota Press: 2013), 42.

12. Weibel, "The Overview Effect and the Ultraview Effect," 12.

13. D. Keltner and J. Haidt, "Approaching Awe, a Moral, Spiritual, and Aesthetic Emotion," *Cognition & Emotion* 17 (2003): 312.

14. Weibel, "The Overview Effect and the Ultraview Effect," 12.

15. Stephanie Nolasco, "William Shatner explains why his trip to space 'felt like a funeral': 'I saw death and I saw life,'" Fox News, October 7, 2022, https://www.foxnews.com/entertainment/william-shatner-explains-trip-space-felt-funeral-saw-death-saw-life.

16. I've written about this in my book: Pasulka, *American Cosmic*, 157.

Chapter 2: Technology and AI

1. Tim Lewis, "'It always hits me hard': how a haunting album helped save the whales," The Guardian, December 6, 2020, https://www.theguardian.com/environment/2020/dec/06/the-songs-that-saved-the-whales.

2. Ibid.

3. Personal correspondence with Australian scientist who wishes to remain anonymous.

4. Tyson Yunkaporta, *Sand Talk* (New York: HarperCollins, 2021), 248, Kindle.

5. Ibid.

6. Ibid.

7. Alexander and Nicole Gratovsky, *The Principle of the Dolphin: Life on the Wave* (Russia: Bombora, 2018).

Chapter 3: The Gray Man

1. Personal communication from Gray Man.

2. Yunkaporta, *Sand Talk* (New York: HarperCollins, 2021), 138.

3. "The Gosford UFO Incident with Moira McGhee," https://www.youtube.com/watch?v=UN_n-jtKMdE; "UFO Gosford," https://www.youtube.com/watch?v=GHQSE2uxDUA. For an excellent overview of this account, see Moira McGhee and Bryan Dickeson, *The Gosford Files—UFOs over the New South Wales Central Coast* (Katoomba, New South Wales: INUFOR, 1996).

4. "The Gosford UFO Incident with Moira McGhee"; "UFO Gosford"; McGhee and Dickeson, *Gosford Files*, 9–13.

5. Personal correspondence with Matthew Roberts, 2021.

Chapter 4: Gray Man II

1. Kary B. Mullis, *Dancing Naked in the Mind Field* (New York: Vintage, 2000): 131–32, Kindle.

2. Project Paperclip.

3. Paul Grigorieff, "The Mittelwerk/Mittelbau/Camp Dora Mittelbau GmbH— Mittelbau KZ: Mittelbau Overview," http://www.v2rocket.com/start/chapters/mittel.html.

4. Craig Marke and Rob Tannenbaum, "Freddy Lives: An Oral History of *A Nightmare on Elm Street*, Vulture, October 20, 2014, https://www.vulture.com/2014/10/nightmare-on-elm-street-oral-history.html.

5. Jacques Vallée discusses the control system. Interview with Jerome Clark, *Fate*, 1978.

6. "Jacques Vallée Discusses UFO Control System," Think About It, https://thinkaboutit.site/ufos/jacques-vallee-discusses-ufo-control-system/.

Chapter 5: The Soldier

1. Pierre Teilhard de Chardin, *The Phenomenon of Man* (New York: Harper Perennial Classics, 2008).

2. Ken Booth, *Theory of World Security* (Cambridge: Cambridge University Press, 2007), 198.

3. Michael Marks, "Drive-By City," *San Antonio Current*, February 24, 2016.

Chapter 6: Gnosis

1. Jacques Vallée, *Forbidden Science 4: The Spring Hill Chronicles* (San Antonio, TX: Anomalist Books, 2019), 439, 440.

2. Ibid., 436.

3. "Esotericism," *New World Encyclopedia*, https://www.newworldencyclopedia.org/entry/Esotericism.

4. Hanegraaff Wouter, *Western Esotericism: A Guide for the Perplexed* (New York: Bloomsbury Academic, 2013).

5. Vallée, *Forbidden Science 4*, 438.

6. Ibid., 126.

7. Ibid., 438.

8. Ibid., 437.

9. Dr. Aaron J. French, "The Magic of Technology: Rudolf Steiner's Rosicrucianism and the UFO Phenomenon," https://www.youtube.com/watch?v=fReIz1gU-nI.

10. Jacques Vallée, *Forbidden Science 4*.

11. Ibid.

12. Ibid.

13. Jacques Vallée, "Jacques Vallee's Stating the Obvious: I, Product," BoingBoing, October 20, 2010, https://boingboing.net/2010/10/20/jacques-vallees-stat.html.

14. Ibid.

15. Personal correspondence with Maria Matsuki Mockett.

Chapter 7: Moon Girl

1. Shawn Eyer, "Translation from Plato's Republic 514b–518d ('Allegory of the Cave')," (Millford, MA: Plumbstone Books, 2016).

2. From an interview with journalist Jeffrey Mishlove, which aired on the PBS series *Thinking Allowed* on April 7, 1997.

Chapter 8: Children of the Invisibles

1. The Space and Missile Systems Center Heritage Center, Los Angeles Air Force Base, CA, https://www.losangeles.spaceforce.mil/About-Us/History -of-SMC/Photo-Page/.

2. "Socrates on the Forgetfulness that Comes with Writing," Work & Days, https://newlearningonline.com/literacies/chapter-1/socrates-on-the-forget fulness-that-comes-with-writing.

Chapter 9: From Atheism to a Magical Mystery Tour

1. As stated in Pasulka, American Cosmic, introduction.

2. All quotes from Len Filppu are from personal correspondence with him.

3. Rochester Democrat and Chronicle, August 3, 1967, 11.

4. Ibid.

5. Rochester Democrat and Chronicle, August 10, 1967, 42.

6. As reported in Pasulka, American Cosmic.

7. https://www.ourstrangeplanet.com/the-san-luis-valley/guest-editorials /jacques-vallee-interview/. Accessed November 15, 2022.

8. Personal communication from Australian scientist.

Chapter 10: The Dream Network

1. Dan Gunderman, "Kurt Russell claims to be pilot who called in pro-lific 1997 'UFO sighting'," New York Daily News, June 16, 2017, https:// www.nydailynews.com/entertainment/movies/kurt-russell-claims-pilot -called-1997-ufo-sighting-article-1.3253058.

2. The following books are excellent analyses of the topic of dreams: Amira Mittermaier, Dreams That Matter: Egyptian Landscapes of the Imagina-tion (Berkeley: University of California Press, 2010); Eric Wargo, Precogni-tive Dreamwork and the Long Self: Interpreting Messages from Your Future (Rochester, NY: Inner Traditions Press, 2021).

3. Jayne Gackenbach and Stephen LaBerge, eds., Conscious Mind, Sleeping Brain: Perspectives on Lucid Dreaming (New York: Plenum Press, 1988), ix.

4. Personal correspondence with Aaron French.

5. Rudolf Steiner, Esoteric Development: Selected Writings and Lectures, https://rsarchive.org/Lectures/EsoDevel/19061020p01.html.

6. Dalai Lama, Sleeping, Dreaming, and Dying (New York: Wisdon Publica-tions, 2002).

7. Yunkaporta, Sand Talk (New York: HarperCollins), 19.

8. Mittermaier, Dreams that Matter, 15.

9. Vincent Crapanzano, *Hermes' Dilemma and Hamlet's Desire: Essays on the Epistemology of Interpretation* (Cambridge, MA: Harvard University Press, 1992), 142.

10. Katy Glaskin, "Innovation and Ancestral Revelation: the Case of Dreams," *The Journal of the Royal Anthropological Institute* 11, no. 2 (2005): 297–314.

11. Douglas Price-Williams and Rosslyn Gaines, "The Dreamtime and Dreams of Northern Australian Aboriginal Artists," *Ethos* 22, no. 3 (1994): 373–88.

12. Personal communication with an archaeologist who wishes to remain anonymous.